China Under Reform

Zhimin Lin

Mason Crest
Philadelphia

CHINa
THE EMERGING SUPERPOWER

China Under Reform

Zhimin Lin

Mason Crest
Philadelphia

Mason Crest
370 Reed Road
Broomall, PA 19008
www.masoncrest.com

CPSIA Compliance Information: Batch #CH2013-3.
For further information, contact Mason Crest at 1-866-MCP-Book.

First printing

1 3 5 7 9 8 6 4 2

Library of Congress Cataloging-in-Publication Data

Lin, Zhimin.
 China under reform / Zhimin Lin.
     p. cm. — (China: the emerging superpower)
 Includes bibliographical references and index.
 ISBN 978-1-4222-2156-3 (hardcover)
 ISBN 978-1-4222-2167-9 (pbk.)
 ISBN 978-1-4222-9445-1 (ebook)
1. China—History—1976-   —Juvenile literature. 2. China—Economic conditions—1976-2000—
Juvenile literature. 3. China—Economic conditions—2000-   —Juvenile literature. 4. China—Social
conditions—1976-2000—Juvenile literature. 5. China—Social conditions—2000-   —Juvenile litera-
ture. I. Title.
 DS779.2.L55 2012
 951.05—dc22
                              2010047755

Table of Contents

Introduction

Dr. Jianwei Wang
University of Wisconsin–Stevens Point

Before his first official visit to the United States in December 2003, Chinese premier Wen Jiabao granted a lengthy interview to the *Washington Post*. In that interview, he observed: "If I can speak very honestly and in a straightforward manner, I would say the understanding of China by some Americans is not as good as the Chinese people's understanding of the United States." Needless to say, Mr. Wen was making a sweeping generalization. From my personal experience and observation, some Americans understand China at least as well as some Chinese understand the United States. But overall there remains some truth in Mr. Wen's remarks. For example, if you visited a typical high school in China, you would probably find that students there know more about the United States than their American counterparts know about China. For one thing, most Chinese teenagers start learning English in high school, while only a very small fraction of American high school students will learn Chinese.

In a sense, the knowledge gap between Americans and Chinese about each other is understandable. For the Chinese, the United States is the most important foreign country, representing not just the most developed economy, unrivaled military might, and the most advanced science and technology, but also a very attractive political and value system, which many Chinese admire. But for Americans, China is merely one of many foreign countries. As citizens of the world's sole superpower, Americans naturally feel less compelled to learn from others. The Communist nature of the Chinese polity also gives many Americans pause. This gap of interest in and motivation to learn about the other side could be easily detected by the mere fact that every year tens of thousands of Chinese young men and women apply for a visa to study in the United States. Many of them decide to stay in this country. In comparison, many fewer Americans want to study in China, let alone live in that remote land.

Nevertheless, for better or worse, China is becoming more and more important to the United States, not just politically and economically, but also culturally. Most notably, the size of the Chinese population in the United States has increased steadily. China-made goods as well as Chinese food have become a part of most Americans' daily life. China is now the second-largest trade partner of the United States and will be a huge market for American goods and services. China is also one of the largest creditors, with about $1 trillion in U.S. government securities. Internationally China could either help or hinder American foreign policy in the United Nations, on issues ranging from North Korea to non-proliferation of weapons of mass destruction. In the last century, misperception of this vast country cost the United States dearly in the Korean War and the Vietnam War. On the issue of Taiwan, China and the United States may once again embark on a collision course if both sides are not careful in handling the dispute. Simply put, the state of U.S.-China relations may well shape the future not just for Americans and Chinese, but for the world at large as well.

The purpose of this series, therefore, is to help high school students form an accurate, comprehensive, and balanced understanding of China, past and present, good and bad, success and failure, potential and limit, and culture and state. At least three major images will emerge from various volumes in this series.

First is the image of traditional China. China has the longest continuous civilization in the world. Thousands of years of history produced a rich and sophisticated cultural heritage that still influences today's China. While this ancient civilization is admired and appreciated by many Chinese as well as foreigners, it can also be heavy baggage that makes progress in China difficult and often very costly. This could partially explain why China, once the most advanced country in the world, fell behind during modern times. Foreign encroachment and domestic trouble often plunged this ancient nation into turmoil and war. National rejuvenation and restoration of the historical greatness is still considered the most important mission for the Chinese people today.

Second is the image of Mao's China. The establishment of the People's Republic of China in 1949 marked a new era in this war-torn land. Initially the Communist regime was quite popular and achieved significant accomplishments by bringing order and stability back to Chinese society. When Mao declared that the "Chinese people stood up" at Tiananmen Square, "the sick man of East Asia" indeed reemerged on the world stage as a united and independent power. Unfortunately, Mao soon plunged the country into endless political campaigns that climaxed in the disastrous Cultural Revolution. China slipped further into political suppression, diplomatic isolation, economic backwardness, and cultural stagnation.

Third is the image of China under reform. Mao's era came to an abrupt end after his death in 1976. Guided by Deng Xiaoping's farsighted and courageous policy of reform and openness, China has experienced earth-shaking changes in the last quarter century. With the adoption of a market economy, in just two decades China transformed itself into a global economic powerhouse. China has also become a full-fledged member of the international community, as exemplified by its return to the United Nations and its accession to the World Trade Organization. Although China is far from being democratic as measured by Western standards, overall it is now a more humane place to live, and the Chinese people have begun to enjoy unprecedented freedom in a wide range of social domains.

These three images of China, strikingly different, are closely related with one another. A more sophisticated and balanced perception of China needs to take into consideration all three images and the process of their evolution from one to another, thus acknowledging the great progress China has made while being fully aware that it still has a long way to go. In my daily contact with Americans, I quite often find that their views of China are based on the image of traditional China and of China under Mao—they either discount or are unaware of the dramatic changes that have taken place. Hopefully this series will allow its readers to observe the following realities about China.

First, China is not black and white, but rather—like the United States—complex and full of contradictions. For such a vast country, one or two negative stories in the media often do not represent the whole picture. Surely the economic reforms have reduced many old problems, but they have also created many new problems. Not all of these problems, however, necessarily prove the guilt of the Communist system. Rather, they may be the result of the very reforms the government has been implementing and of the painful transition from one system to another. Those who would view China through a single lens will never fully grasp the complexity of that country.

Second, China is not static. Changes are taking place in China every day. Anyone who lived through Mao's period can attest to how big the changes have been. Every time I return to China, I discover something new. Some things have changed for the better, others for the worse. The point I want to make is that today's China is a very dynamic society. But the development in China has its own pace and logic. The momentum of changes comes largely from within rather than from without. Americans can facilitate but not dictate such changes.

Third, China is neither a paradise nor a hell. Economically China is still a developing country with a very low per capita GDP because of its huge population. As the Chinese premier put it, China may take another 100 years to catch up with the United States. China's political system remains authoritarian and can be repressive and arbitrary. Chinese people still do not have as much freedom as American people enjoy, particularly when it comes to expressing opposition to the government. So China is certainly not an ideal society, as its leaders used to believe (or at least declare). Yet the Chinese people as a whole are much better off today than they were 25 years ago, both economically and politically. Chinese authorities were fond of telling the Chinese people that Americans lived in an abyss of misery. Now every Chinese knows that this is nonsense. It is equally ridiculous to think of the Chinese in a similar way.

Finally, China is both different from and similar to the United States. It is true that the two countries differ greatly in terms of political and social systems and cultural tradition. But it is also true that China's program of reform and openness has made these two societies much more similar. China is largely imitating the United States in many aspects. One can easily detect the convergence of the two societies in terms of popular culture, values, and lifestyle by walking on the streets of Chinese cities like Shanghai. With ever-growing economic and other functional interactions, the two countries have also become increasingly interdependent. That said, it is naïve to expect that China will become another United States. Even if China becomes a democracy one day, these two great nations may still not see eye to eye on many issues.

Understanding an ancient civilization and a gigantic country such as China is always a challenge. If this series kindles readers' interest in China and provides them with systematic information and thoughtful perspectives, thus assisting their formation of an informed and realistic image of this fascinating country, I am sure the authors of this series will feel much rewarded.

Foreign businessmen walk past booths at the Canton Trade Fair in Guangzhou, China. By the mid-1970s China was struggling economically, its people among the poorest in the world. Since 1978 a program of reforms has enabled the country's economy to grow at an average annual rate exceeding 8 percent, the fastest growth rate in the world during that period.

Overview: The Landscape of China's Reform

One of the most important global developments during the last decades of the 20th century was the rise of China as a world power. After two and a half decades of growth averaging more than 8 percent annually, China's economy by 2003 had become the second largest in the world, as measured by purchasing power parity (PPP). (PPP is a method of calculating economic output that minimizes the influence of short-term currency fluctuations, which can skew the figures.) From 1990 to 2009, China's total exports grew from about $62 billion to more than $1.2 trillion. In 2000 China's share of total global exports was still under 4 percent; by 2009 that share had jumped to more than 9.5 percent. China's economy, in the words of economists David Hale and Lyric Hughes Hale, has simply "taken off."

Members of a Revolution Committee paint anti-capitalist slogans on banners, circa 1967. The Cultural Revolution was directed at intellectuals and people in authority deemed to have capitalist leanings. By the time it ended in 1976, the economic and social structure of Chinese society had been devastated.

Accompanying China's newfound economic importance is a more assertive stance on the world stage. In recent years, China has played an increasingly active role in a wide range of international issues, from the fight against terrorism to peace on the Korean Peninsula to economic cooperation in the Asia-Pacific region. China entered the World Trade Organization (WTO), the highest regulatory body for international trade, in 2001. It hosted the Summer Olympics in Beijing in 2008 and the World Expo in Shanghai in 2010. Chinese leaders travel all over the world more and more frequently. Since being forced to open its doors to the West in the mid-19th century, China—the former "sick man" of Asia—has never had more influence in international affairs.

The rise of China is even more impressive when one compares China's recent experience with that of other developing nations such as India. In 1980, for example, India's population stood at 687 million, and its gross domestic product (GDP) per capita—essentially the average share of each Indian in the country's total economic output—was $1,400 (based on PPP). China, on the other hand, had more than 1 billion people and a GDP per capita of less than $800. By 2011, however, India's population had risen to about 1.2 billion and its GDP per capita to $3,700, whereas China, with a population of 1.35 billion, boasted a GDP per capita of $8,400. Both China and India have made great strides in reducing the number of people living in poverty. But China has gone much further. Since 1979 China has lifted 400 million of its citizens out of poverty and reduced the overall poverty rate to around 13 percent. India, on the other hand, still has a poverty rate hovering at 25 percent.

The success of China's economy can be explained first and foremost by the massive economic reforms it has undertaken since 1978. These reforms have touched upon virtually every aspect of life in China. For anyone who wishes to understand how China has become what it is today, and to glimpse what the future might hold for the world's most populous nation, a clear understanding of the reform movement is a must.

Origins and Nature of the Reforms

China's recent reform movement started less than two years after the death of Mao Zedong (1893–1976). One of the most radical leaders of the 20th century, Mao was responsible for the founding of the People's Republic of China in 1949. He was also responsible for many disastrous political campaigns, such as the Great Leap Forward (1958–1960) and the Cultural Revolution (1966–1976). By the time of his death in 1976, Mao's policies had reduced the country to ruins. Clearly, China was in urgent need of some fundamental changes.

However, what direction these changes should take and how they should be implemented were by no means self-evident immediately after Mao's death. It was not until late 1978, when Deng Xiaoping (1904–1997) emerged as the top leader of China, that the country firmly embarked on a sweeping reform movement. A veteran Communist, Deng had joined the revolution in the late 1920s. But Deng was considerably more open-minded and practical in his approach than was Mao. During his youth, he traveled to France and saw firsthand the large gap between China and the West. During the Cultural Revolution, Deng himself was purged and sent to do manual labor in a tractor factory. These experiences convinced him that Mao's utopian socialist policies would not work in China.

After he returned to power, Deng introduced one reform after another, never looking back. He first dropped the emphasis on political ideology and instead called on the nation to embrace economic development as the number one priority. He began to replace the old Soviet model of a centralized, planned economy with practices that were more characteristic of a market economy, such as competition, pricing based on supply and demand, and incentives for good performance. He aban-

Mao Zedong (left) and Deng Xiaoping examine a letter. After Mao's death, Deng emerged as the leader of China and oversaw a gradual program of economic reforms.

doned Mao's policy of self-isolation and introduced an "open-door" policy designed to encourage the inflow of foreign investment, technology, and managerial expertise into China. Finally, he dropped Mao's call for global revolution in favor of a new foreign policy aimed at achieving a peaceful international environment in which China could concentrate on economic modernization.

Deng called his new policies "socialism with Chinese characteristics." Ordinary Chinese, however, saw the reforms more as a golden opportunity to improve their living standards and pursue personal advancement. After more than two decades of economic hardship and political fear under Mao, they were more than ready for a change, particularly one that might yield tangible results. They grabbed Deng's call for reform with unprecedented energy, enthusiasm, and creativity. Before long, Deng's reform programs had begun to produce some early signs of success: fresh produce began to reappear in the stores; wages, which had been frozen for years, began to go up; Chinese universities resumed the practice of admitting students based on their exam scores, after a 10-year lapse; and people started to taste greater personal freedom, as restrictions on travel and employment were effectively lifted.

In the former Soviet Union and many of the countries of Eastern Europe, the transition from communism toward a market-based economy came with enormous social trauma and economic pains, at least initially. By contrast, Deng's reform program in China resulted in much less social disturbance, and it produced material benefits that average citizens could feel directly. As a result, overall support for reform has, from the beginning, remained strong, despite significant ups and downs along the way. Indeed, the thrust of China's reform efforts—a relentless nationwide pursuit of economic growth—has never been altered. This consistency of focus, along with the cumulative gains that have sustained and even accelerated the momentum for reform, goes a long way toward explaining how China has outperformed other states that have undertaken similar reforms, some of which began the process with greater expectations.

Reform Without a Blueprint

China's march toward economic reform was in part fueled by strong leadership and popular support. But success or failure was ultimately linked to how the reform program was executed.

Even a casual observer will note several interesting features of the reform process in China. Most conspicuously, it proceeded with neither a blueprint nor an overarching plan (unlike reform undertaken in Russia and in many other former Communist states). Instead, the Chinese reforms were based on two general practices. First, Deng and his successors deliberately chose an incremental approach to push forward their reform programs. Deng once compared China's reform process to someone who wants to cross a river but does not know how deep the water is: before taking each step, he carefully uses his toe to feel for stones. Since there was no precedent, Deng argued, China's reform process must advance one step at a time and on a trial-and-error basis. More controversial was the second general practice: putting economic growth ahead of political liberalization (which further distinguished reform in China from reform in the Soviet Union under Mikhail Gorbachev). Development, Deng argued, must be considered the sole firm objective because only by sharply improving living standards could the government gain the support of its people. Deng viewed Western-style democracy as a ticket to chaos and hence to be avoided at all costs. Deng did not reject political reform per se; he simply believed that economic reform must take precedence, and he was determined to block any political changes that might threaten the conditions he considered necessary for economic progress, such as stability.

Three Phases of Reform

China's quarter century of reform can be divided into three phases. During the first phase (1978–1984), the government used a land lease system known as the Rural Household Responsibility System to free hundreds of millions of Chinese peasants from the failed collective system (also called the commune system). The results were overwhelming. Within five years, Chinese agricultural output doubled, and many Chinese farmers became enthusiastic supporters of the reform movement. Deng showed similar decisiveness on a number of other reform programs, such as the open-door policy and the reorientation of China's foreign policy.

However, Deng's response to the popular call for greater political openness and democracy was much more ambiguous. On the one hand, even Deng recognized that China's existing political system was flawed and must be modified to prevent a repetition of such tragedies as the Cultural Revolution. So certain reform measures, including elimination of lifelong tenure for Communist leaders and preliminary efforts to establish the rule of law, were adopted. On the other hand, Chinese leaders showed little hesitation to crack down when they perceived a threat to Communist rule. For example, the Chinese government during this period crushed the famous Democracy Wall Movement and launched a number of campaigns to suppress calls for liberalization in the arts and literature.

As China entered the second phase (1984–1989) of reform, the impact of Deng's pragmatic and incremental approach could be seen even more clearly. During this period, Deng tried to expand economic reform to China's cities. Instead of pushing for more radical methods such as a large-scale privatization, the Chinese leaders opted for a so-called dual-track system. Under this system, the state would encourage the development of the private sector and the use of market mechanisms such as supply and demand to determine some prices. At the same time, the state would maintain a large public sector and retain control over some key economic activities. The hope was that the private sector would, over time, outgrow the public sector—but without the large-scale disruption that would likely occur if privatization were adopted overnight.

However, dismantling the old system turned out to be far more difficult in the cities than in the countryside. Resistance to reform was particularly strong among the bureaucrats. While the dual-track system provided some cushion against the backlash caused by the reforms, it created other problems. A jump in inflation and loss of jobs alienated many city residents. Moreover, the loopholes in the new system made it easier for corrupt officials to take advantage of the power they held at the expense of the public. Many of these problems could have been mitigated if not solved had China adopted some fundamental political reforms, such as the establishment of a system of checks and balances and an open press. Deng would allow neither, however.

In spring 1989, university students in Beijing, angered by the rise of official corruption and frustrated by the lack of political reforms, staged a two-month-long pro-democracy demonstration at the heart of China's capital. Tensions escalated, and both the demonstrators and the government failed to take advantage of opportunities to avoid a violent confrontation. Finally, on the night of June 3–4, the government crushed the student movement with force. The Tiananmen massacre became the most tragic incident of the Chinese reform era.

After the crackdown, the Chinese reform process entered its third phase. Political reform, which had been extremely limited to begin with, was shelved through the 1990s. Economic reform, however, kept moving forward. In 1992, in his last major public act, Deng went to southern China to inspect the special economic zones that he had helped set up in the early years of reform to encourage foreign investment and experiment with capitalism. During his tour,

Although Deng and other Chinese leaders permitted greater economic freedom, they stifled attempts to move the country toward democracy. In June 1989, government troops brutally crushed a pro-democracy demonstration in Beijing's Tiananmen Square. This video image shows a lone demonstrator attempting to block a column of tanks from entering the square.

he called on the country to accelerate economic reform and seek faster growth. Since then, Deng's successors have followed in his footsteps by expanding economic reforms in several key areas. Together, these expanded reforms have created what some have called "the third revolution"—in which reform is no longer focused on correcting past mistakes but more on a systemic effort to build a comprehensive and true market economy.

On top of these reforms came the decision to formally accept private ownership as a legitimate part of the economy and to encourage the private sector to become the dominant force in China's growth. In the 1990s, the structure of China's economy shifted decisively to favor the non-state-owned sectors. China also moved to establish and strengthen various markets to provide a platform for market-based competition. As a result, goods, information, and money are now flowing fairly freely through the vibrant operations of the labor market, capital market, real estate market, and numerous commodity markets. Some of these markets are still rudimentary by world standards; other markets, however, have become quite sophisticated.

A key component of economic reform has been the effort to integrate China into the global economy. Many barriers to free trade with other countries have been removed, particularly since China's 2001 entry into the WTO. As a result, China has become a favorite site for foreign investment and trade. In fact, since 1997 China has received more direct foreign investment than all nations except the United States, and Chinese-made goods can be found virtually everywhere in the world.

Reforms have recently taken place even in the social policy and political areas. China has greatly increased investment in education, information technology, and science. In 1978 China reintroduced the university entrance examination system; today its universities boast the second-largest enrollment in the world and produce the largest number of engineers. The government has also introduced numerous reforms to reinvent many social programs. For example, in the public health care area, a new system based on social insurance has been established to replace the old system in which the state provided health care directly. And because employment is no longer guaranteed by the state, a new social security system has been introduced. Many cities have adopted a minimum income standard to protect low-income families. On the political front, some long-postponed reforms were introduced in the early years of the 21st century. Competitive elections at the village level were first permitted in 1988. Ten years later, voters in Buyun township, Sichuan Province, directly elected the township magistrate. That led hopes for more extensive, bottom-up democratization.

Since the late 1970s, China has greatly increased its investment in education. As a result, Chinese universities boast the second-largest enrollment in the world.

Those hopes, however, have remained mostly unfulfilled.

The most recent revision of the Chinese constitution, adopted in 2004, formally offers protection for private property and human rights. But such guarantees have thus far meant little in practice. Local and provincial Communist Party officials are notorious for forcing peasants from their land in order to make way for development projects in which the officials have a personal financial interest. Graft, bribery, embezzlement, and other forms of government malfeasance are so widespread that President Hu Jintao felt compelled to issue a warning to Communist Party members in 2011, on the occasion of the 90th anniversary of the party's founding. "Corruption," Hu said, "will cost the party the support and trust of the people." Meanwhile, China's human rights record remains dismal, according to various international organizations.

Reform in China is still unfolding. However, its impact on domestic as well as international developments has been significant. The next five chapters will examine some of the most important areas of reform and assess the successes as well as the remaining problems.

A Chinese peasant works in a rice field. Until relatively recently, the majority of China's people were poor farmers living in rural areas.

2

Changes in Rural China

China's economic reforms started in the vast countryside. This was no coincidence. Until recently, a large majority of Chinese lived in rural areas, and agriculture had long been the most pivotal sector of the economy. Throughout Chinese history, the well-being of the peasants played a key role in the rise and fall of political regimes and in social changes. This time it was no different. As David Zweig, a longtime student of Chinese agriculture, put it, "One of five people in the world lives in rural China. Given the magnitude of China's population, what happens to China's farmers has tremendous implications, not just for urban China or China's ambitious reform programs, but for the entire world."

This Chinese poster from 1956 describes a 10-year plan for the development of agriculture in the country. The illustrations show Mao Zedong in a meeting, peasants in a field with a poster of Mao, two people with vegetables, and a man on horseback with a herd of horses.

From Communes to Rural Households

The reform movement that swept the entire nation had its roots in a failed system introduced by Mao in rural China. In 1958, as part of his Great Leap Forward campaign, Mao launched the people's commune movement. In less than a year, the new commune system was firmly established; it served as the basic framework for rural Chinese life. Consisting of about 5,000 households on average, the communes were a key part of Mao's ambitious plan to turn China into a Communist society. Under the commune system, private ownership of land and most property would be replaced by collective ownership. Members of a commune would work together, sharing whatever products they collectively produced. But the communes were more than economic entities. Politically, they governed on behalf of the state. Top commune officials, who were appointed by the government, answered to the Communist Party and the state. And socially, the communes replaced many functions traditionally reserved for families or individuals. For example, they ran nurseries, nursing homes, clinics, and schools.

The commune system, though utopian in design, proved a costly failure in practice. As hundreds of millions of peasants were forced into some 24,000 communes nationwide, they were cut off from their traditional links to farming. They lost all decision-making power in production. They were subject to arbitrary rules set by the local leaders. Because output was divided equally among all members of the group (after the state took its portion), there was little incentive for individuals to improve their productivity or to introduce innovations in farming. Not surprisingly, this type of organization became a major drag on economic development in rural China. Grain production, for example, stagnated in the years following the introduction of the commune system. With more than 85 percent of its labor force working in the fields, China still faced severe and chronic shortages in its food supply and in the supply of most farm products. In one of the most visible signs of the failure of Maoism in agriculture, the state after the Great Leap Forward had to impose a strict ration system limiting the amount of staple goods such as rice, meat, and cooking oil that urban residents could purchase.

But it was China's peasants who bore the brunt of Mao's policy failures. In the wake of the Great Leap Forward, China experienced one of the worst famines in world history. An estimated 20 million to 30 million Chinese lost their lives, and most of these deaths occurred in the countryside. The commune system did other, less obvious harm to China's peasants, however. In place of the separate, traditional villages in which they had lived for generations, peasants found themselves in large and hierarchically organized communes, where virtually all aspects of their lives were regulated by Communist Party managers. Not only were traditional social ties destroyed, but Mao was able to mobilize the peasants for his frequent political campaigns, repeatedly disrupting their normal production. By the time Mao's era drew to a close, China's peasants had been impoverished and thoroughly demoralized by his disastrous policies.

Chinese farmers work together in one of their commune's fields. The commune system, introduced by Mao Zedong in the 1950s, proved to be an inefficient failure.

In 1979, shortly after Deng and other reform leaders took control, desperate peasants from some of the poorest parts of the country began to experiment with a new farming system on their own initiative. Defying government regulations, they secretly decided to carve up the collective land into small pieces and have each of these pieces cultivated by a single family. The gamble quickly paid big dividends, as production in these villages soared. Word of the villagers' success spread fast, and soon peasants from all over the country were demanding the right to adopt a similar system. By summer 1981, more than 95 percent of the rural areas in China had adopted some form of contracting land to individual households.

Impressed by the results, the new Chinese leadership led by Deng moved decisively to abandon the commune system. It replaced the communes with a new system known as the Rural Household Responsibility System. Under this system, the state would lease parcels of land (the land is still collectively owned according to the law) to individual households for up to 15 years (the lease was extended to 30 years or longer in 1994). The peasants would agree to pay government taxes and allow the state to procure a portion of their products at a set price. But beyond that, they were free not only to cultivate the land as they saw fit (choosing, for example, how to allocate their labor and which crops to grow) but also to dispose of surplus produce as they wished (consuming it personally or selling it to earn extra income, for instance). The land could also be inherited or subleased.

This change in property rights was the catalyst for the fundamental transformation that has swept rural China over the last three decades. While not billed as privatization per se, the new land lease system nevertheless created an operational approach in rural China that in many ways was parallel to a private farming system. For example, the new arrangements allowed the peasants rather than the state to make decisions regarding the use of the land they leased. To do well, peasants had to compete in the marketplace. The more they produced, the more income they could take in. In the words of a well-known Chinese expert, the new system has essentially "turned the 200 million or so rural households into 200 million small but independent enterprises."

The new system thus helped to unleash the long pent-up energy of the Chinese farmers. Millions of them used the new opportunities to increase crop yields, expand production, and provide better products and more variety to the market. From 1979 to 1989, the gross output of farming and other related industries grew by more than 75 percent in inflation-adjusted prices. The annual growth rate reached 5.77 percent for the period, the highest in post-1949 China. In the process, more than 100 million Chinese farmers moved out of poverty. The net income of Chinese peasants rose from 200 yuan per person in 1980 to more than 600 yuan in 1990.

A woman selling fresh produce waits for customers at a stand near Shanghai. The Rural Household Responsibility System, implemented in the early 1980s, encouraged Chinese farmers to become more efficient; it permitted them to earn extra money by selling their surplus crops.

Entering the 1990s, however, the process of reform in rural China had become more complex and challenging. The initial force of reform had already been brought to bear. The central concern of many peasants was no longer subsistence but rather the possibility of sustained growth and prosperity. In response to the changed environment and expectations, Chinese leaders have in recent years concentrated on several fronts in order to advance a new round of reforms in rural China.

"De-agriculturalization"

One such effort sought to raise rural incomes by broadening the work performed by peasants beyond agricultural production. In

China arable land is scarce, and the average rural household leases less than an acre from the state. If many members of a family are working to cultivate the same small farm, much of their labor is essentially wasted; beyond a certain point, the land cannot be made to yield more crops, and the value of, say, a bushel of wheat remains the same regardless of how many worker-hours were spent cultivating it. To increase the productivity of the rural workforce (and thus rural incomes), it is necessary to move "surplus labor" out of farming and into other lines of employment (preferably without completely detaching these workers from their rural roots).

This process, known as "de-agriculturalization" (*Fei Nonghua* in Chinese), has several key components. The early post-Mao reform period saw an explosive growth of rural-based factories, known as township enterprises. In the 1990s this trend continued, as upwards of 100 million former peasants gained employment in more than 20 million township enterprises. These enterprises collectively accounted for one-fourth of China's GDP. But more important, they provided critical employment opportunities for former peasants, and wages earned in these jobs became a major source of income for many rural families.

An equally large number of farmers have migrated to China's large and medium-sized cities for jobs. By 2009, according to China's State Population and Family Planning Commission, these migrant peasants (known as the "floating population") numbered 211 million, more than 15 percent of China's total population. Some are seasonal workers; others have established a more permanent presence in the cities and travel back to their home villages only during the holidays (officially they are not counted as urban residents, however). This unprecedented rural-urban migration has had a significant impact on development in rural China. While many of the migrant workers live in miserable conditions and face all sorts of discrimination in the cities, some nevertheless manage to send much-

Migrant workers carry their possessions in a Beijing street. According to official Chinese government data, more than 210 million Chinese travel between rural and urban areas to find work.

needed cash to their families in the countryside, and they serve as conduits of information between urban and rural China.

For those who remain in the countryside working the fields, significant changes have come as well. For instance, the government has encouraged farmers to sublet land, in the hope that those who cultivate larger pieces of land can achieve greater efficiency and better returns through economies of scale (reductions in unit cost associated with larger-size enterprises). In 1994 alone, one-tenth of the total leased land changed hands.

The "de-agriculturalization" process has had a profound impact on the shape of Chinese agriculture. The overall number of peasants has remained steady, but the percentage of them engaging in actual farming has declined dramatically, from 78 percent in 1990 to less then 40 percent by the early years of the 21st century. The share of rural income from farming has also declined dramatically, to less than 20 percent. If this trend continues, the image of

China as a predominantly agrarian society will soon become a thing of the past.

Moving Peasants into Towns and Cities

Another effort by the state was to relocate more peasants into towns and small cities. This move was intended to serve several purposes. It would help accelerate the process of industrialization and urbanization, both of which were long viewed as key to China's modernization. It would also help improve the living conditions and boost the consumption level of the peasants. Finally, it would make providing social services to the rural population easier. In 1978 there were fewer than 3,000 towns in the entire nation; by 1998 the number stood at almost 17,000. Some of the towns or small cities, especially those in or near coastal areas, have since grown into modern urban centers. And the number of residents in towns and cities throughout the country surpassed 690 million by 2011.

There was a second front in this effort. As part of the enormous process of urbanization occurring in China, the state encouraged major urban centers to incorporate adjacent rural areas into their city limits. Through administrative redistricting, the state also placed most rural counties under the management of a central city. The hope was that integrating cities and the surrounding rural areas would create a "spillover" effect that would hasten development in rural China.

Building a Market System for the Rural Economy

Finally, the state made concerted efforts to build a comprehensive market system as the leading mechanism for the rural economy. This market-oriented approach had a number of facets. The first was a fast expansion of the private sector and private ownership. During the first decade of reform, for example, a majority of the township enterprises were still owned by the collective body—townships—that replaced the communes. After the mid-1990s, most of these enterprises were either sold or leased to private investors, and some have grown into large conglomerates that play an important role not only in rural China but also in the cities.

To nurture the growth of the market system, the state deliberately withdrew from a number of areas in which it previously exercised direct control. For instance, the government stopped issuing procurement quotes (by which households were obliged to sell grain to the government at a certain price) in rural areas. Instead, it used commercial contracts to purchase grain and other products from the farmers or, in some instances, simply purchased them directly from the markets. Most of the exchanges in rural areas were now based on supply and demand. Government intervention in the market was basically limited to instances in which steep price increases or decreases might threaten the economic well-being of peasants.

Widening Gaps

More than two decades of reforms have paved the way for a higher standard of living in rural China; issues such as basic subsistence have largely been solved for most Chinese farmers. At the same time, many serious problems remain, and reform leaders now find themselves confronting challenges that touch upon the very core of the Chinese system.

One such challenge is severe income disparity. The gaps between rural and urban areas, between peasants in different regions, and between farmers and non-farmers have grown to the point that, if left unattended, they could seriously undermine—if not completely derail—the reform process.

A recent study by the United Nations found that the ratio of average family income in urban China to average family income in rural China exceeded 3:1. In other words, the typical city-dwelling family earned more than three times as much as their rural counterpart. This disparity is among the highest in the world. (And if the numerous welfare benefits received by city residents were taken into account, the disparity would be even greater.) A similar rural-urban divide was seen in education. Researchers found that for every 10 youth from the cities who entered college, only one from the rural areas did so. The gap between peasants in rich and poor areas was also growing. For example, the average income in rural areas along the more prosperous coastal region was more than twice that in the less developed western region. Even within the same locality, average income for peasants in traditional farming might be a small fraction of average income for peasants in non-farm work.

A significant rise in income disparity is not unusual during the early stages of a country's transition from a government-controlled command economy to a market economy. But the widening gaps in China could signal long-term problems—and have, in fact, already had negative consequences on efforts to reduce poverty. In 2003, according to the Chinese government, the number of rural residents living in abject poverty increased by about 800,000—marking the first time that poverty had risen since the beginning of the country's economic reforms 25 years earlier.

High-rise apartments loom just beyond a grain field; the irrigation ditch in the foreground is littered with garbage. As China's cities have grown larger, absorbing adjacent rural areas, millions of acres of arable land have been lost to development.

Despite substantial gains by many rural residents over that period, an estimated 30 million peasants were still living in abject poverty, and there were another 60 million whose income was extremely low even by Chinese standards. Most of these peasants lived in poor regions (such as the west) and relied on traditional farming as their sole source of income. The chances for these people to find support and move beyond poverty are dim unless the overall disparities between rural and urban areas and between different regions are reduced.

The widening gap between rural and urban areas has created another dilemma. On the one hand, the future growth of China's economy depends on a healthy agricultural sector to serve as both

A Chinese man collects bottles and cans to sell for recycling. In 2003 China recorded its first increase in the number of people living in absolute poverty since the beginning of the reform period a quarter-century earlier.

a key producer and a big consumer market. On the other hand, if the rural-urban divide persists or grows, more and more human talent, capital, and other resources will flee the impoverished rural areas, thus making the situation even worse. Breaking this vicious circle will be crucial to the long-term health of China's economy.

Weak Rural Institutions

An even more fundamental problem is the lack of rural institutions to safeguard the progress made under the name of economic reform, protect the rights of average farmers, and ensure the long-term interests of rural communities. To be fair, attempts were made after the breakup of the commune system to reinvent compatible local institutions. Township government now serves as the basic unit of government. In 1988 the state introduced village-level elections to select village heads. More recently, there have been sporadic efforts to expand such elections to the township level. Similarly, several new laws, including the 2002 Land Contract Law, have been adopted to provide a legal framework for dealing with various disputes or to provide guidance for various relationships in rural China.

Yet despite these efforts, rural institutions remain particularly weak and out of step with the fast pace of China's economic reforms. For example, corrupt local officials have in many instances swallowed up most or all of the financial gains peasants have made under rural reform. Peasants have in recent years complained of the increasingly burdensome taxes and fees imposed on them by local officials—despite the fact that the central government has several times ordered that such levies be reduced. Unfortunately, local officials are able to act with virtual impunity because of a lack of institutional checks and balances at the local level. In one of the most popular books published in 2004, two Chinese reporters spent three years documenting case after case of abhorrent violations by local officials against defenseless peasants. The book provoked strong public outrage, but similar abuses have continued to occur.

The root cause of this problem, of course, lies in the one-party system. The Communist Party maintains a monopoly of state power, and it has always been wary of creating alternative institutions that might threaten this position. The very nature of the recent Chinese reforms did not help either. The emphasis on economic but not political reform created a rich soil in which bureaucratic abuse, corruption, and violations of individual rights flourished. But while the Communist Party has balked at creating institutions that might act as counterweights to its power, the lack of such institutions in rural areas could undermine the very economic reforms Chinese leaders want to pursue. In recent years there has been a sharp rise in street demonstrations and violence on the part of peasants outraged by the arbitrary seizure of their homes and other property or by their high taxes. Bureaucratic mismanagement and the absence of effective supervision have caused another set of problems. A recent study, for example, found that almost 80 percent of the rural counties and townships were deep in red ink. Their cumulative debt was estimated as high as 50 percent of China's GDP. In either case, time is running out for Chinese leaders to create effective rural institutions to deal with these problems.

Lack of Social Services

With the exception of a few better-off rural districts, most of the rural areas in China today lack basic social services, and this too poses a threat to the future of reform and economic development. The status of public health care illustrates just how serious the problem is. Under the commune system, public health care was provided through a rudimentary but useable system of collective care. After the commune system was abolished in the early 1980s, the collective care system was also abandoned. However, for almost two decades, the state failed to establish an alternative health care system.

By the end of the 1980s, more than 90 percent of the rural population had to use out-of-pocket money to pay for doctor visits and drugs. In the period 1990–1999, when the average net income of peasants doubled, the costs of doctor visits and hospitalization rose more than six times. As a result, a growing number of peasants could not afford even the most basic health care. Moreover, the 1990s saw a sharp rise in AIDS, tuberculosis, and other diseases, most often in the poorest rural areas.

In response to the emerging crisis in public health, the Chinese government has adopted a number of measures, including several models of health insurance, over the last few years. It is too early to tell whether these measures alone can solve the problems and truly meet the needs of the peasants.

Conclusion

In general, the introduction of the Rural Household Responsibility System has changed rural China for the better. It gave hundreds of millions of peasants control over the land they worked and the freedom to seek wealth. In a country where for thousands of years the distribution of land was always at the center of government control, this was no small achievement. On the other hand, the changes in land distribution alone cannot guarantee either long-term prosperity or social stability. Whether or not rural China continues to experience overall progress will depend on how—and how well—the state addresses the deeply rooted structural issues discussed in this chapter.

A busy terminal filled with shipping containers in Yantian International Port, Shenzhen. Deng Xiaoping's economic reform program called for improving Chinese industry and technology.

3

Changes in Urban China

When economic reform spread to China's cities in the mid-1980s, the challenges presented were very different from, and far more complex than, the obstacles to reform in the countryside. Despite the fact that only a small proportion of the population (17.9 percent in 1978) lived in urban centers, the cities hosted almost all of China's important political, economic, and educational institutions. They served as the nerve centers for the country's industrial, commercial, and cultural activities. In rural China a single bold measure—the Rural Household Responsibility System—had effected a quick turnaround. In urban China reform proceeded more slowly, as leaders were fearful of triggering social unrest and severe economic dislocations. Moreover, urban reform happened at a time when not one but three fundamental transformations were taking place in China simultaneously: urbanization, industrialization, and marketization. Balancing competing needs and managing the process would require that leaders adopt a different strategy for urban reform from the one used in reforming China's rural areas.

Breakup of the Old System

The first task of urban reform was to undo the old Soviet-style, centralized planning system. Under this system, the state owned most economic entities (with the exception of some small businesses) and gave production quotas to its state-owned enterprises (SOEs) following annual and long-term economic plans. Government agencies controlled the price as well as the flow of most goods. They set wages and benefits for managers and workers alike. Investment decisions, which were based on the priorities perceived by the state, seldom reflected the needs of the public or the true costs and benefits. Under Mao's policy of self-reliance, trade with foreign countries was minuscule, and the channels linking China with the outside world were limited.

In addition to owning most of the enterprises, the state, through a hierarchical chain of command, controlled the welfare and, by extension, the political loyalty of the employees of the SOEs. Until recently, most Chinese workers were assigned to a job, and they worked for a company for life. In addition to guaranteed employment, known as the "iron rice bowl," workers received cost-free benefits such as health care, education, and retirement benefits from their employer. Under such a system, Chinese workers were not only highly immobile but also highly dependent on their employers and, by extension, the state.

So when Deng and other Chinese leaders tried to introduce reform into the cities, they were faced with a dilemma. On the one hand, they had no choice but to abandon the current economic system. After more than two decades of central planning and the disruptive influence of Mao's continual political campaigns, China's economy was in shambles. On the other hand, Deng did not have a free hand to reform as he saw fit. For ideological reasons, some approaches, such as wholesale privatization, were essentially off limits. More important, Deng and other Chinese leaders worried about how workers would react if, as part of the reforms, they lost the jobs and the welfare benefits that were guaranteed them under the old system.

Deng and his associates decided to proceed cautiously with urban reform. They employed a three-prong strategy that, they

In 1980 China's government designated five areas as "special economic zones." The goals of these zones included attracting foreign investment and technology, as well as increasing China's exports of finished goods. The program was so successful that new zones were created over the next 15 years; pictured here is the Pudong Special Economic Zone, which was opened to foreign investment in 1990.

hoped, would help generate enough momentum for reform but defuse opposition and spread the risks. First, they adopted a dual-track system to dismantle the old system incrementally. For an extended period, the state would retain control of most SOEs, as well as the prices and distribution of basic materials and critical commodities. Meanwhile, the state would use policy incentives to encourage the growth of non-state sectors and expand the use of market mechanisms such as supply and demand in allocating resources. Deng and his colleagues hoped that under this gradualist approach, the private sector and market forces would slowly outgrow the public sector, without the massive shock to the Chinese people that would accompany a rapid and comprehensive reform effort.

The second prong of China's urban reform strategy was the open-door policy, which was championed especially by Deng. Deng used the policy to achieve several goals: attracting much-needed foreign investment, technology, and managerial skills; bringing in new ideas; and loosening the grip of the bureaucracy by exposing China's economy to world standards. To that end, Deng quickly and completely abandoned Mao's policy of self-reliance. He sent thousands of Chinese intellectuals to Western countries to absorb new information and ideas. He also set up several special economic zones (SEZs) near Hong Kong to allow unfettered experimentation with capitalism, and he then used the SEZs to showcase the alternative to central planning.

The third prong of China's urban reform strategy was decentralization, which Deng used to bypass expected resistance from China's entrenched bureaucracy. Under the slogan "streamlining governance and decentralizing power," Deng gave local officials greater decision-making authority on such critical issues as investment, tax collection, and economic regulations. These decentralization measures often involved little transfer of fiscal resources from the central to local governments. But they helped Deng win the support of local officials while at the same time providing the more open-minded of these officials with incentives and space to introduce innovative reform measures and seek better ways to boost local economic growth.

This three-prong strategy helped China outperform economically other former Communist states by a large margin. In Russia, for example, the Boris Yeltsin government (1992–1999) adopted a "big bang" approach to economic reform that included a massive privatization scheme and the freeing of prices overnight. The result of this approach was a decade-long depression that cut the Russian economy by more than half. By contrast, China's economy enjoyed 30 years of uninterrupted growth averaging more than 8 percent annually.

Homeless Russians wait in line for a meal served by a charity in Moscow. The success of China's economic transition stood in stark contrast to the problems experienced by Russia and other former Communist countries in Eastern Europe and Central Asia.

But Deng's reform strategy for urban China was not without its share of problems. In particular, the dual-track system created considerable confusion for ordinary citizens and much room for official corruption. Many government officials blatantly used their positions of power to exploit loopholes in and between the two systems for personal gain. The massive student movement that broke out in Beijing and many other Chinese cities in 1989 was fueled largely by growing public anger at this rampant corruption, along with the runaway inflation made possible, if not caused, by Deng's partial reforms.

Urban Reform in the 1990s

The 1989 student movement revealed the limits of the dual-track system. To regain popular support after the bloody crackdown and to avoid a similar uprising in the future, the new Chinese leadership searched desperately for a new strategy. Once again, Deng came to the rescue. In spring 1992 Deng, who had theoretically retired from his official posts in November 1989, made a highly publicized tour of southern China, including some of his favorite SEZs. During the trip, Deng called on the nation to accelerate economic reform. He insisted that there should be no boundaries, ideological or policy-related, to confine reform and economic growth. "Those who do not support reform must go," he reportedly warned.

Deng's calls touched off a second wave of reform in urban China that was in many ways more momentous than the first wave of reform of the 1980s. Guiding this second phase of reform was a substantially revised reform strategy. For example, the new strategy no longer centered on how to undo the mistakes of the past. Instead, it committed the nation to the establishment of a full market system. The new strategy also made modernizing Chinese cities, especially their infrastructure, a top priority. Advocates argued that this was the only way to breathe new life into China's declining urban centers and to stimulate growth. Finally, the revised reform strategy called for a new round of industrialization based on international standards and closer integration with the world economy.

Like the reform of the 1980s, the 1990s' version did not have a carefully designed blueprint. Instead, it was more or less an article of faith among top Communist Party leaders that the only way to maintain the legitimacy of a government so badly bruised by the events of 1989 was through faster economic growth and the delivery of tangible benefits to the people. Beginning in the early 1990s, the leadership basically decided to let Chinese citizens do whatever they wanted in making money—as long as they did not challenge the power of the state or the legitimacy of the Party. Some called this a grand but nevertheless short-term "bargain" between the state and the public; others argued that this represented a turning point in the relationship between the government and the people. Whatever the interpretation, the new strategy played an important role in the tremendous economic transformation that swept much of urban China during the 1990s and continued into the new millennium.

Shortly after Deng's tour in 1992, the Chinese government formally announced that it would embrace a full market economy. There was no inconsistency, according to the official statement, between a market-based economic system and socialist goals. The announcement ended several years of debate over the issue. It also opened a floodgate of new initiatives and reforms designed to build a comprehensive and functional market system.

Privatization Without the Name

Among the initiatives was an effort to privatize a large portion of the economy. On paper, the government still refused to call the move privatization, instead using the term *Gaizhi* (change in ownership system). In practice, the lack of a formal name made no difference. The privatization took several forms. First, the government sold off most small SOEs outright. For the remaining SOEs, the government took a three-step approach. The central government would continue to control some 500 of the largest and most strategically important companies. The local governments, which managed the rest of the SOEs, were given greater latitude in deciding the future of these companies. For example, they could liquidate money-losing enterprises, merge such enterprises with more profitable companies, form large business groups to achieve economies of scale, or lease or sell the companies to private investors. Finally, the large SOEs that remained under the control of the central government would gradually be converted into share-holding companies and, when feasible, listed on local or international stock markets.

As a result of these measures, the number of SOEs declined by more than 88,000, or 33 percent, between 1997 and 2001. The non-state sectors of the economy, by contrast, grew by leaps and bounds. In 2002 non-state-owned companies accounted for more than 65 percent of China's GDP, 69 percent of all urban employment, and more than 53 percent of total investment.

A Vibrant Private Sector

To build a full market economy, the state finally committed itself to allowing the private sector to be a dominant player in the marketplace. Before 1992 there had already been considerable growth in the private sector. But the process was uneven and subject to periodic backtracking. Deng's southern tour in 1992 helped remove the lid on private-sector development. Explosive growth in privately owned companies followed, especially in the areas of construction, real estate, export-oriented industry, and retail. In more recent years, the growth of private businesses has further expanded into such areas as education, financial institutions, and even health care. Meanwhile, private companies are no longer small or marginal players in the market. Some have emerged as enormous conglomerates controlling large market shares and huge financial resources. For example, a recently formed investment group in Zhejiang, a prosperous province near Shanghai, had combined assets reportedly worth $60 billion.

Institutionalizing the Markets

Efforts to build markets in China started in the mid-1980s, but it was not until a decade later that such efforts were extended to virtually every sector of the economy. Today, a full range of markets (including stock markets, real estate markets, and numerous commodity markets) exists in China. In 2012, for example, more than 2,400 Chinese companies were listed on China's two stock exchanges, with a combined market capitalization of more than

Chinese investors track prices on an electronic board at the stock exchange in Beijing. By 2012 more than 2,400 Chinese companies were listed on China's two stock exchanges.

$3.3 trillion. The market-centered system has become so pervasive that the Chinese government now requires most government procurement to be done through bidding in open markets.

Urbanization and Urban Renewal

The campaign to create a full market economy played a large role in the recent boom in urban China, but other forces were at work as well. In fact, a more direct contributor to the economic upsurge in the cities was the massive process of urbanization and urban renewal, which dramatically changed the landscape of urban China. From 1949 to the late 1970s, the Chinese government for political and security reasons discouraged the growth of the cities. Not only were peasants strictly prohibited from migrating to the cities, but the government also made little investment in the basic infrastructure of urban China. During the first decade of reform, the government loosened the ban on rural-urban migration, yet because of a lack of budgetary resources, only limited urban renovation and renewal occurred. As recently as the early 1990s, much of urban China was bedeviled by crumbling roads, overcrowded living space, outdated transportation systems, and poor management.

The situation began to change dramatically after the government took several bold and creative measures to expedite urban renewal. One of the measures was to lease the right to use urban land to real estate developers or to investors interested in public-works projects such as highways. By doing so, the government killed three birds with one stone. First, the receipts from land leasing and the flood of investment money pouring in helped finance mammoth projects the government could not previously afford. Second, the value of the leased land went up sharply, boosting not only the real estate market but also the construction industry and related businesses, which directly benefited the local economy. Third, city residents could see visible improvements in their living conditions, winning support for the government's reform agenda.

Efforts to modernize the cities received another critical boost when the Chinese government decided to privatize the urban housing sector in the mid-1990s. Until then, housing in urban areas had been treated as part of the welfare benefits workers received from the state. The government owned the apartment units, and the residents paid only nominal rent. There was a chronic shortage of housing, and existing units were poorly maintained. In 1994 the government decided to privatize public housing. Existing housing units would be sold to the tenants; new units would have to be purchased at market prices. Many observers consider the privatization of housing one of the most far-reaching decisions in the whole urban reform process. Like the leasing of land to rural households, the privatization of housing turned urban residents into instant property owners. Every city resident now had a stake in the outcome of urban reform, which made them natural allies in the reform process as they sought to protect their property or increase their wealth.

In the space of a single generation, China has been transformed from a predominantly rural to a substantially urban society—and the process of urbanization is only accelerating. In the late 1970s, less than 20 percent of China's population lived in cities or towns. By 2012 more than half of China's 1.35 billion people were urban residents.

It is hard to overestimate the profound changes wrought by massive urban renewal and massive urbanization, twin processes that have fueled one another. Shanghai provides perhaps the most illustrative example. Before 1991 this city's nickname, "the Paris of the East," was an embarrassment, for while Shanghai was China's most sophisticated and cosmopolitan city, it was nevertheless a run-down backwater. In fact, one foreign reporter visiting the city in 1991 remarked that it seemed as if World War II had just ended.

Shenzhen, 1995: Old buildings are in the process of being demolished as new skyscrapers rise in the background. Urban renewal and expansion programs have greatly changed the face of China since the early 1990s.

Today, after more than 15 years of frantic construction, Shanghai boasts well over 2,000 skyscrapers, and this bustling financial and commercial center is the equal of any world-class city. Urban renewal projects and the rapid expansion of China's cities created a large number of jobs, attracting millions of migrant peasants looking for a better life. This virtually unlimited supply of inexpensive labor, in turn, further hastened urban renewal.

A New Wave of Industrialization

In the early 1990s the Chinese government concluded that to ensure continued economic expansion in the long term, new "growth poles"—particularly in high technology—would have to be found. (Growth poles are key industries that spur the development of related businesses, employment, and secondary economic activity.) The government also recognized that for China to compete in international markets, it would have to upgrade critical industries to bring them into conformity with international standards. These initiatives sparked a new round of industrialization, especially in the more prosperous coastal and select inland regions.

The new industrialization centered on three large undertakings. First, extensive efforts were made to bring new technologies to China, develop domestic high-tech industries, and upgrade the infrastructure so that China would be both a major producer and user of high-tech products. As part of this initiative, the central government and local governments offered financing, technical assistance, tax breaks, and other monetary and policy incentives to attract investment in high-tech research facilities and production lines. Second, the government used industrial policy and other measures to encourage the expansion of traditional industries, such as the steel and chemical industries, as well as new industries, such as automobile manufacturing and pharmaceuticals. Finally, the

A woman assembles a switchboard in the Alcatel telephone factory, Pudong Special Economic Zone. China's program of economic reform focused on attracting and developing high-tech industries.

government made the development of export-oriented industries a major priority.

The second round of industrialization has produced impressive results. Industrial production continues to drive China's economic growth. In 2011, for example, industrial production grew by nearly 14 percent, while GDP increased by more than 9 percent. The new round of industrialization also provided new job opportunities. This was particularly important as the added jobs helped offset the loss of jobs in many of the traditional industries.

As China's new industrial revolution took off, growing amounts of foreign investment flowed into the country, and more manufacturing facilities were built. Perhaps it is still too early to call China the "world's manufacturing floor," but there is no disputing the fact that China is an increasingly important player in world manufacturing output—as well as a large market for manufactured goods. From 1978 to 2002, China attracted $500 billion in foreign direct investment (FDI), 10 times the total Japan accumulated between 1945 and 2000. In 2003, for the first time, China replaced the United States as the largest recipient of FDI. With the external help, China has become one of the world's major exporters of industrial goods.

Challenges and Solutions

China's three-prong reform strategy helped the country grow out of its post-1989 slump, then spurred the enormous boom in urban China in the 1990s. Entering the new millennium, the trends continued to point to expanded reform in Chinese cities and more integration into the world economy, especially with China's entrance into the WTO in 2001. On the flip side, after three decades of fast growth and expansion, urban China has begun to face problems that can no longer be solved by short-term fixes. Some of the problems are by-products of the recent economic boom; others are long-term and structural in nature. Whatever the origin, these problems have become a serious threat to the continuation of growth and improvement in urban China.

One of China's most serious problems is environmental degradation, and this has affected the cities as well as the countryside. In 1998 the World Health Organization reported that 7 of the 10 most polluted cities in the world were in China. Over the past two decades, bad air quality alone has caused more than 2 million deaths.

In addition to environmental degradation, the development of urban China has also run into several critical bottlenecks. Chinese cities now face serious shortages in the supply of clean water. Land available for urban expansion has become increasingly scarce as well. And China's urban boom has been sustained by overseas sources of energy, raw materials, and industrial goods, making the country more vulnerable to the fluctuations of the world market.

Growing unemployment is another big problem. Economic restructuring (and particularly the bankruptcy of many state-owned enterprises) has cost more and more urban residents their jobs. Gone forever is the "iron rice bowl" of the Mao era. The official unemployment rate for city residents increased from 3.1 percent in 1999 to 4.1 percent in 2012. However, accounting for laid-off workers who had not yet officially been registered as unemployed, the actual 2012 urban unemployment rate might have been closer to 6 or 7 percent, and various Western economists place the number as high as 10 percent. The loss of jobs caused widespread resentment and even ignited sporadic protests in cities and towns. Many Chinese list unemployment as one of the top issues the country must address if it is to avoid serious social repercussions.

Even in areas in which urban China has made great strides, deeply rooted problems remain. For example, the second wave of industrialization turned China into a fierce competitor in world

A layer of slime and garbage floats on the surface of Hong Kong's Victoria Harbor. The rapid growth of Chinese industries has had an unwanted side effect—rampant environmental pollution.

markets, but China still relied heavily on technology imported from other countries. The growth of service industries was not able to keep pace with industrial development, leaving China behind not only the United States and Japan in this category, but also India. Similarly, while urban renewal and the improvement of urban infrastructure have been two bright spots in China's recent development, much of the expansion has been financed through a sharp increase in bank loans. This raises serious questions as to what will happen to the boom in many Chinese cities if the economic situation forces Chinese banks—which are already troubled by bad loans—to scale back investment.

Can urban China handle these problems? To be sure, the reform process in China has never been problem free. In theory, there is no reason to suppose that China cannot deal with these problems, given its record in addressing other serious challenges, such as the post-1989 recovery. However, as many observers point out, the root of many problems in urban China is more political than economic. For example, the central government's overwhelming emphasis on economic growth led many local officials to pay lip service to environmental protection. Similarly, China's oil consumption has surged in the last decade, turning the country from a net exporter of crude oil as late as 1993 to the world's largest importer in 2011. Many factors contributed to this turnaround. However, the combination of the government's decision to promote automobile manufacturing as a leading industry and its failure to take effective measures to increase energy efficiency was no doubt a primary factor. In the end, whether or not urban China can sustain robust growth depends heavily on how well the Chinese government adjusts its policies.

A Chinese family, photographed on an outing to a science museum. Historically, the family was the basis of Chinese society, but the role of the family and other traditional institutions was weakened during Mao Zedong's rule.

4

Reform and Social Changes

Until China's reluctant entry into the modern age beginning in the mid-19th century, the Chinese culture and civilization had displayed remarkable coherence and resilience in the face of numerous civil wars, natural disasters, and internal political upheavals. At the core of the civilization was a social structure built on a strong role played by the family, an emphasis on moral behavior through education and based on the teachings of Confucius, a "weak" class system, and a political culture that valued groups more than individuals and favored submission to authority over independence.

Chinese Society on the Eve of Reform

With the arrival of the Europeans and China's defeat in the Opium War (1839–1842), the once invincible

"Middle Kingdom" began to crumble, creating an unprecedented crisis for the traditional Chinese society. Under the slogan of "using Western learning for practical development but keeping Chinese learning as the essence," some limited reform was introduced in the late 19th century to salvage the imperial system and to reform the traditional society. However, such efforts proved to be too little and too late. Not only did the imperial system collapse in 1911, but also growing numbers of social movements directly challenged the wisdom of China's traditional norms. One of these movements, the famous May 4th Movement of 1919, went so far as to call for the overturning of the Confucianism-based orthodoxy. To survive in the face of Western powers, China needed "Mr. S" (science) and "Mr. D" (democracy), declared the leaders of this movement.

British warships destroy Chinese junks in this engraving of a battle from the Opium War (1839–42). During the 19th century, Britain and other European nations humbled the Chinese military and forced the emperors to agree to humiliating and unfair treaties.

When Mao and the Chinese Communist Party (CCP) claimed victory in China in 1949, their vision for a new Chinese society, and their efforts to create such a society, continued the assault on the traditional Chinese values and social structure. It is true that Mao's ideology took certain pages from the Chinese tradition. For example, the Chinese tradition emphasized moral behavior through learning, and Mao's revolution likewise stressed the need to educate the people about "correct" behavior. Overall, however, Mao's radical ideology and policies shook the very foundation of Chinese society and Chinese culture as never before.

By the 1970s Chinese society was in a state of deep turmoil. Mao's political campaigns had weakened the most important institution in traditional Chinese society: the family. With Mao's campaigns pitting one family member against another, the Chinese family lost its time-honored role in establishing the structure of authority, offering moral upbringing to children, and providing ultimate support for family members in times of crisis. Under Mao the traditional role of intellectuals in Chinese society—to provide moral guidance for political rulers and advise against any behavior inconsistent with the ethical standards set forth by Confucianism—was also lost. Mao's anti-establishment and anti-elite bias demoralized and politically marginalized China's intellectuals. Worst of all, the traditional value system that formed the foundation of Chinese society was greatly shaken. First indoctrinated by Maoism and then, as Mao's revolutionary experiment unraveled, deeply disillusioned by it, many Chinese were at a loss as to what to believe.

Social Consequences of Post-Mao Reform

Against this social background, the post-Mao reforms sent shock waves through Chinese society and forced it to adjust. Some of the adjustments helped to restore pillars that had supported the traditional Chinese society but were severely eroded under Mao. For example, education, a prime target for Maoist attack, quickly regained its prominence. Indeed, one of Deng's first reforms was to reintroduce a nationwide examination system to select college students, a move that boosted the morale of China's intellectuals and reconfirmed the value of learning. The emphasis on education continued throughout the reform period and even gathered steam as the government started an ambitious program to expand higher education in order to ensure future economic development. Many parents, better off financially in the wake of the reforms, were more than willing to invest in their children through education. As a result, college enrollment in China soared, from 2 million in 1990 to 4 million in 1999 to more than 10.5 million in 2012. At least in

A group of Chinese schoolchildren. Renewed emphasis on education was one of Deng Xiaoping's first priorities, and it has helped fuel China's economic growth.

this area, the forces unleashed by the economic reforms seem to have matched perfectly with the traditional belief in education as the key to success, for the individual or for society as a whole.

But the social impact of the recent reforms went far beyond repairing or restoring the traditional order. In fact, because of its revolutionary nature and unprecedented reach, the reform agenda actually poses more long-term challenges to traditional Chinese society than Mao ever did. For example, the reforms have unleashed a relentless drive to seek personal wealth, which has fundamentally altered the dynamics of Chinese society. The reforms have paved the way for a freer flow of information and direct contact with the outside world, rendering obsolete the traditionally inward-looking orientation of Chinese society. Economic reforms have also spurred significant shifts in China's population. Changes in jobs, income, and living standards—along with increasing social mobility, including the massive rural-urban migration—have made family ties less stable. They have also called into question the traditional norms that guided interpersonal relationships for centuries. It is still too early to evaluate the full impact of the reforms on Chinese society, but the evidence so far suggests that changes are wide-ranging and fundamental.

Income Gap and Social Division

Historically, Confucianism and China's other leading ideologies always downplayed the importance of material wealth in determining social status. Mao's revolution further stressed the merits of an egalitarian society. The recent economic reforms moved China in a very different direction, however. First, there was a fundamental shift in government philosophy and policy regarding income distribution. For example, Deng abandoned Mao's egalitarian policies altogether, believing that they produced nothing but poverty for all. To stimulate the economy, he called for "letting a few people become rich first." Private ownership, denounced by Mao throughout his entire rule, flourished under the encouragement of the reform government. In March 2004 China's parliament, the National People's Congress, approved a constitutional amendment that obliged the state to "respect and protect private ownership."

More important, China's economic boom has brought an explosive growth of personal wealth. One particularly visible sign of the increased prosperity is a dramatic rise in the number of automobiles seen on China's streets. Not too long ago, access to a car was a perk reserved for top Communist Party officials; car ownership was a luxury not simply beyond the means, but beyond even the dreams, of ordinary Chinese. By 2010 China had surpassed the United States to become the world's largest automobile market.

But the growth in individual wealth has been accompanied by a sharp increase in income inequality, and this holds true for virtually every category. As mentioned in chapter 2, in China the income gap between rural and urban residents is now the highest in the world. In 2007, according to official Chinese government statistics, urban dwellers made 3.3 times more income per person than rural residents. There is also an enlarging income gap between the more prosperous coastal areas and the less developed inland and western regions. To address this problem, President Hu Jintao promoted large-scale investment in rural infrastructure and other development projects. But the resulting influx of migrants from eastern China stoked social unrest among ethnic minority groups in areas such as Inner Mongolia and Xinjiang.

A considerable and growing income gap also exists among different professions. For example, the average monthly salary for a blue-collar worker in a coastal city might be just 10 percent of the salary commanded by a professional working for a multinational corporation. According to a recent study, the top 10 percent of families in urban China now control more than 45 percent of the total assets, while the bottom 10 percent share less than 1.5 percent.

Heavy traffic clogs highways in Beijing. Greater prosperity has made it possible for more Chinese to own cars; by 2010 the country had become the world's largest automobile market.

Some observers view the growing income gap as a necessary price for modernization. Others are more concerned about the negative consequences on Chinese society. For example, in a recent survey of local officials, more than 78 percent said that China had entered a period of social instability. They pointed to the rise of official corruption and the accelerating income gap as two key factors contributing to the trend.

A recent study by leading Chinese sociologists revealed the emergence of social divisions based on income—which to a Westerner might seem unremarkable but which historically has not been characteristic of Chinese culture. While the authors did not believe that China's social stratification was unusual for a modernizing state, they did warn of potentially serious consequences if the divisions became wider or if too many people stayed in the lower social groups. The authors found that the lower the social group, the more negatively its members viewed the effects of China's reforms. For example, industrial workers as a group had particularly strong objections to the growing income gap in the country.

However, another recent study suggests that the negative effects of the spike in income inequality may be somewhat tempered by several developments. For example, growing home ownership has elevated more Chinese into the so-called middle-income group. According to official government statistics, about 23 percent of China's population fell into this group in 2012. The growing middle class, some have argued, provides the best hope for China to avoid the kind of severe social disruption that many former Communist countries have experienced.

Social Problems and Tensions

If the income gap and the emergence of a social-class-based society are principally signs of structural transformation in China, the rise of social problems and tensions constitutes a more immediate challenge to the reform movement. China over the last three decades has seen a sharp increase in social problems linked to the changes brought about by reform efforts. Reliable crime statistics for China aren't available, but the government does acknowledge that the total number of crimes committed has doubled since the 1990s. Still, most experts believe that the crime rate in China is low when compared with the crime rate in many Western countries.

Corruption remains a significant—and evidently growing—problem. That fact was illustrated in dramatic fashion in 2012, with the downfall of Bo Xilai. Bo, the Communist Party's leading official in Chongqing, was believed to be in line for China's top internal-security post. But after Bo's wife was implicated in the suspected mur-

A Chinese policeman transports a handcuffed thief on a motorbike in downtown Shanghai. While promoting reforms, China's government is also coping with an increase in crime and other social problems.

der of a British businessman, a web of corrupt dealings involving Bo came to light. He was sacked, and the scandal threatened to end the careers of other top Communist Party officials as well.

Tempted by the huge amounts of money now flowing through the economy, along with a general lack of oversight, more and more officials—from local functionaries all the way to leaders in the central government—have been caught for embezzlement, bribery, and misappropriation of public funds for personal use. The direct economic loss from official corruption is estimated at more than 1 percent of China's GDP annually.

Other forms of crime have spread during the reform period as well, reflecting a deteriorating social order. By 2001 the government was concerned enough about the rise of organized crime to launch a nationwide crackdown. Drug trafficking and use have also surged. In 2009 there were more than 1.2 million drug users registered for treatment in China—which, experts believe, represents a small fraction of the actual number of addicts—and the numbers are expected to rise even further. Thus far, China's anti-drug campaigns have apparently failed to make a dent in either the supply of, or the demand for, illegal drugs. Prostitution and many other forms of profit-driven social vice have also made a big comeback in the last two decades.

The economic reform has created space (and sometimes even incentives) for the rise of social ills. Until 1988 China had only a few dozen cases of AIDS. In 2011 the Chinese government reported nearly 800,000 registered HIV carriers and AIDS patients. The actual number of HIV/AIDS cases is probably considerably higher, and infection rates are expected to rise substantially in coming years.

A student carries an AIDS awareness placard during an event held in Beijing for World AIDS Day. Since the late 1980s, the number of people in China infected with HIV, the virus that causes AIDS, has exploded.

Food safety has recently become a major public concern in China, as numerous cases have been reported of food being produced using substandard materials—or even being mixed with poisonous chemicals. The motive in such cases has invariably been the desire to make a quick profit.

Recent social changes have generated wealth for many Chinese, but they have also left others impoverished, exploited, and cut off from traditional social support systems. The Chinese media popularized the term *vulnerable groups* to refer to those in society who are most susceptible to abuse or exploitation; these groups include homeless children, women from abusive families, elderly people deserted by their children, and child laborers, among others. With the number of people in these groups on the rise, and their plight increasingly an issue of major concern, the term *vulnerable groups* has even entered official publications.

Perhaps the most serious challenge to the future of reform, however, comes from rising social tensions stemming from abuses perpetrated by government officials, from failed public policies, or from a combination of the two. In the last few years, two issues have elicited particularly strong public reactions. In rural China, especially in the poorer regions, local officials have forced many farmers to pay excessive taxes and fees, even though the central government has issued numerous directives to reduce or even ban such burdens on low-income peasants. In the cities (and, to a lesser extent, in rural China as well), the arbitrary seizure of residents' homes to make way for new housing or commercial projects has sparked public outrage and even violent protests. In the face of such confrontations, local officials typically resort to silencing the opposition through the use of the state apparatus, including local militias, rather than through negotiations.

In the face of rapid and profound social and economic changes, Chinese society faces a fundamental question: What should be the moral underpinning of the nation? While economic reform has successfully unleashed market forces and created opportunities for personal advancement, it has so far failed to offer an alternative value system to replace the one that has been swept aside. Several competing sources have attempted to fill this moral vacuum by advancing a belief system that might serve as the backbone of China's much-changed society.

Official Responses

From the founding of the People's Republic of China in 1949, Communist ideology—as adapted by Mao—served as an overarching (and officially enforced) belief system. Yet the post-Mao reforms largely entailed an abandonment of Maoist and Communist theory and goals. Recognizing the dangers of a vacuum in belief, Chinese leaders have continued to portray their policies in the language of socialism and communism—even when the terms used no longer bear much connection with their original meanings. They have also introduced new theories and concepts that attempt to refashion Communist ideology in such a way that the CCP can continue to claim moral leadership and legitimacy as China's ruling party. One recent attempt in this regard was the "Three Represents" theory, introduced by the CCP in 2001 and ultimately written into China's constitution. Instead of identifying itself with such traditional Communist goals as public ownership and a classless society, the CCP claimed that what made it the natural leader of the country was that the Party represented "the requirements of the development of advanced productive forces, the orientation of the development of China's advanced culture, and the fundamental interests of the overwhelming majority of the people in China."

Through this rather ambiguous statement the CCP was hoping to rally public support and to create enough space for it to adjust to the changed socioeconomic conditions without openly abandoning the ideological goals originally enunciated by Mao. Under this revised interpretation of the CCP's mission, for example, even private businessmen (the "advanced production forces" alluded to in the Three Represents) were now welcome to join the CCP; previously entrepreneurs had been reviled as enemies of communism. Similarly, the Chinese government has increasingly relied on populist and nationalist themes to justify government actions or gain public support. So far, however, the Chinese government's efforts to regain the moral high ground have met with only limited success, as these efforts have largely been undermined by rampant corruption and widespread abuse of power on the part of government officials.

Religious Revival

In China, a historically secular state, religion has played a less prominent role than in many other countries. A few religions, especially Buddhism, were accepted or even extolled by political and civil leaders as moral guides. But in the absence of an officially sanctioned religion or a state church, Confucianism became a dominant political philosophy and a sort of secular religion. Inspired by and named after the philosopher Confucius (551–479 B.C.), Confucianism attracted Chinese rulers and common people alike largely because of its accessibility and its rich and practical discussions of the human world of families and states rather than the more impenetrable world of gods and spirits. Through *Analects*, a compilation of Confucius's teachings, and the writings of other prominent Confucian figures such as Mencius (ca. 371–ca. 289 B.C.), Confucianism became the primary source of moral guidance, the foundation for training government officials (its texts long formed the basis of China's civil service examinations), and inspiration for intellectual debate and inquiry. Later, other religions such as Islam and Christianity spread to China too, although their influence was more limited to certain geographic areas, ethnic groups, or social groups.

Religion and religious activities were effectively banned under Mao; following in the footsteps of Karl Marx, the chairman rejected religion as the "opiate of the people"—even though he had no problem with being elevated into a god-like figure himself. After Mao's death and the launching of the economic reforms, China has seen a visible, albeit still small, religious revival. One researcher recently wrote, "On any given Sunday, there are almost certainly more Protestants in church in China than in all of Europe." According to official figures, there are more than 100,000 churches, temples, and mosques in China. Estimates place the number of people in China

Chinese Catholics line up to receive Communion during Christmas Mass at the Wangfujing Catholic Church in Beijing. The practice of religion was banned under Mao Zedong; since his death, China has experienced a limited but noticeable religious revival.

considered "religious" at more than 100 million, a figure that is up sharply in recent years. Among them are more than 10 million Protestants, 4 million Catholics, and 18 million Muslims. More than 30 million copies of the Bible have been printed and distributed in China since the late 1980s, not including millions more that were smuggled into China. Even in Beijing, politically the most controlled city in China, there are 10 Catholic churches, 8 Christian churches, 10 temples dedicated to Lamaism (the form of Buddhism prevalent in Tibet), and 70 mosques. In addition, some people in Beijing and elsewhere throughout China attend house church or other forms of religious gathering not approved by the state. Taking into account these people, whose numbers are difficult to measure, up to 10 percent of China's total population might be considered religious.

Overall, however, religion has so far not been able to supplant the official ideology. Religious activities in general are subject to strict limitations imposed by the state. All public religious organizations must register with the government, and their activities are closely monitored. Religious organizations are allowed to provide only limited services and are prohibited from openly engaging in any political activities. Even church-sponsored charity activities are subject to severe restrictions for fear they might assume the state's role.

Cases of religious persecution have been reported with some frequency. Anyone who seeks independence from state control of religion, organizes underground religious activities, or simply pushes religious activities beyond the "red line" drawn by the state risks punishment. On the other hand, the government's efforts to control religion do not always work. Occasionally, harsh treatment of religious associations or figures has backfired, causing strong resistance—as the government's attempts to suppress the spiritual movement known as Falun Gong demonstrate.

In addition to organized religion, other forces have flowed into the vacuum in belief systems created by the reform movement. Various philosophies, popular culture movements, folk religions, and cults have competed for the hearts and minds of ordinary people. Consumerism has had a clear and lasting impact on the values of Chinese society; other trends have come and gone. It remains to be seen whether a single belief system will again predominate as Confucianism and communism once did.

Population Policy, Family, and Beyond

In the early 1970s, in order to curb runaway population growth, the Chinese government began encouraging its citizens to have fewer children. By 1980 the government had formally adopted a controversial policy by which couples were permitted to have only one child (under special circumstances, and with government approval, a couple might be allowed to have a second child, but never a third). Compliance was obtained through monetary incentives and penalties, as well as more coercive means.

The implementation of the "one-child" policy helped reduce the fertility rate from 5.4 children born per woman in the 1970s to 1.8 children born per woman by the end of the 20th century. This reduced rate accounted for some 300 million fewer births from the early 1970s to the beginning of the 21st century. A number of international organizations, including the United Nations, regarded China's population policy as one of the most effective programs among Third World countries.

Almost from the beginning, however, China's population policy came under heavy attack. Critics assailed not only the inflexibility of the official policy but also the harsh enforcement methods adopted by many local officials, which contributed to widespread abuses. Such abuses ranged from the use of threat and coercion to forced abortions and sterilization (and even, in some cases, infanticide).

The one-child policy has also generated unintended consequences that may well come back to haunt China in the long run.
In fact, some of these consequences are already evident.
Because of the longstanding cultural preference for male children, many Chinese couples chose to abort female fetuses rather
than have the only child they were permitted be a girl. This has
led to a younger population composed of significantly more
males than females. One result is that many men, particularly in
rural areas, cannot find marriage partners.

Another potentially troublesome consequence of the one-child
policy is that China is fast becoming an aging society (defined as
a society in which the proportion of people 65 years and older
exceeds 10 percent of the total population). In some places, such
as Shanghai, that line has already been crossed. And it is project-
ed that China as a whole will join the ranks of aging societies by
the year 2020. Under the economic reforms, health care costs
and retirement benefits are no longer paid by state-owned enterprises. The question is, therefore, how will China pay these sky-
rocketing costs?

One solution would be to relax population policy, as more people in the workforce would generate more wealth, and a portion of
that increased wealth could fund the benefits of older people.
Interestingly, the success of China's economic reforms may
already have resulted in a more varied pattern of population
growth, irrespective of government policy: as incomes went up,
monetary rewards and punishments became less effective in con-
vincing couples to abide by the one-child policy, and the increased
mobility of the population, especially the rural population, made
individuals' compliance with the government regulations difficult
if not impossible to monitor. Yet in certain locales, officials have
deliberately relaxed the government's longtime population policy.
In Shanghai, for example, the local government recently decided

控制人口数量
提高人口素质

计划生育

Pedestrians walk past a billboard promoting China's one-child policy; the slogan reads, "Control population growth, and raise the quality of the population." China's policy has succeeded in slowing the growth of the country's population, but it has also had several unintended consequences, one of which is that China is becoming an aging society.

to allow people who remarried to have a second child. Other localities went even further. In some of the richest rural towns in Zhejiang, for instance, local governments openly gave approval for families to have a second child. Some even provided incentives for families to do so, as long as they promised not to migrate to another area. All in all, about 600 counties—representing half of China's 1.35 billion people—have adopted more liberal rules on birthrates.

The combined force of the population policy and changing socioeconomic conditions resulting from the reforms has led to some fundamental changes in family relationships in China. The traditional Chinese household tended to be a close-knit extended family in which the authority of parents was unquestioned. Today, however, nuclear families make up the majority of households in China's cities. Even in rural areas, where extended families remain more common, the trend is toward smaller households as there are fewer young people—and even fewer decide to stay in the villages. In addition, family relationships are no longer universally hierarchical, with the younger generation obeying the will of the older generation. Nor are family ties as close as they were before. This is due in part to economic changes and in part to a growing generation gap regarding virtually every topic touching on family, including marriage, sex, spending habits, and friendship. In a recent study, for example, less than 10 percent of college freshmen listed their purpose in entering college as "realizing the expectation of parents." Almost 80 percent listed "getting an ideal job or personal advancement" as their goal.

Thousands of pro-democracy supporters march in Hong Kong to commemorate the victims of the 1989 Tiananmen Square massacre. Despite some recent progress, most observers agree that China has a long way to go toward an open, democratic system.

5

Political Reform

China's enormous economic and social transformations have put the spotlight on the question of democracy. If democracy is understood in terms of a multiparty system and a representative government chosen through free popular elections, then clearly there is no democracy in China as of this writing. The question is, what are the prospects for democratization in China? Will the forces unleashed by the economic reforms be powerful enough to move China away from the current authoritarian regime and closer to a democratic form of government?

The transition from absolutism to democracy may be a long and multifaceted process involving incrementally greater political participation, a more diverse distribution of political authority, and a more pluralistic society. Seen from this perspective, China, it might be argued, has already begun the process of democratization—

though precisely where that process will lead, or how far it will ultimately go, is difficult to say. This chapter examines the recent changes (or the lack thereof) in China in four areas that are commonly viewed as crucial to any democracy: basic rights and freedom, the rule of law, competitive elections, and a strong civil society. It argues that the cumulative effects of the changes in these areas indicate that China is not only moving toward a more democratic system but has a good chance of seeing that trend continue and expand in the wake of the recent economic reforms.

China's Political System Under Mao

The recent movement toward a more democratic system in China took place against the backdrop of a political system that had been dominated by Mao for more than two decades. Under Mao, the Chinese system had two competing faces. On the one side, it resembled a typical Stalinist state. One party, the Chinese Communist Party, held the monopoly of power. Decisions by the CCP and its leaders were final as there was neither a system of checks and balances nor an independent judiciary. Consequently, there was no room for such concepts as the rule of law or human rights. The state was the final arbiter of right or wrong. It dominated the society, controlling not only the behavior but also the thinking of its citizens. In this sense, Mao's China could be called a totalitarian system (one in which state control is complete), as opposed to a more conventional authoritarian system, in which the government exercises arbitrary rule over political life but leaves substantial space for private and business life.

On the other side, Mao's China differed from a typical Stalinist state such as the former Soviet Union in several important ways. Most Stalinist states relied on secret police and the direct use of the state apparatus to suppress opposition. Mao, by contrast, enlisted direct public participation in his revolutionary experiments. He even allowed the Chinese people to bypass the state apparatus and launch their own political initiatives. In certain respects the political power of the state depended more on Mao's charisma and cult of personality than on bureaucratic institutions. In addition, because of Mao's constant political campaigns, the chains of command and political boundaries were less stable; they were subject to constant revision and differing interpretations, thus leaving room for political factions to flourish.

This dual face of Mao's political legacy had a major impact on the reforms that began after his death. In contrast with reforms in the Soviet Union, which were initiated by the leadership and carried out in a top-down fashion, important reform programs in China (such as the Rural Household Responsibility System) were started from the

Chinese citizens surf the internet in a café in Chengdu, 2011. Today nearly 500 million Chinese have regular access to the internet, although the Chinese government maintains a strict regime of online censorship. This effort includes tracking and arresting dissident bloggers; blocking foreign news sites and a long list of search terms, including "freedom," "democracy," and "Tiananmen Square massacre"; and banning popular platforms such as YouTube, Twitter, and Facebook.

bottom up and only later recognized by the state. Even with reforms that were directed by the central government, local discretion often made the implementation of changes less uniform than the central government had hoped.

Mao's legacy had another far-reaching impact on political reform in China. At the chairman's death, the bureaucracy stood weakened and demoralized by his relentless political campaigns. But the excesses and horrors of Maoism—including the chairman's last disastrous experiment, the Cultural Revolution—had also produced a populace that was quite leery of radical change. Under Mao, attempts to transform Chinese society had invariably ended in widespread suffering and social chaos. No one was anxious to repeat those experiences. So while the Chinese people in the wake of Mao's death may have welcomed democratic reforms, the vast majority was unwilling to risk more instability in the name of political change.

Deng: In Pursuit of Limited Reform

Reflecting this complex heritage from the Maoist era, the post-Mao leadership under Deng launched a partial political reform. Deng's goal was threefold. First, he clearly wanted to put in place a system that would prevent unlimited political power from again residing in the hands of a single leader, which he believed had enabled Mao's excesses. Thus Deng championed the abolishment of the life-tenure system for top CCP leaders and institutionalized a decision-making process oriented more toward collective leadership. Second, Deng wanted to reinvent the government system so that it would become more efficient and capable of serving the needs of economic development. Several rounds of reforms were aimed at reducing the size of the central government and streamlining its work, giving more power to local governments, and establishing channels that would make government officials at all levels more responsive to popular demands. Third, Deng took several steps to rearrange the overall political system in order to protect the changes that took place under his reign. For example, he called for the establishment of the rule of law to handle political and economic conflicts. He favored more separation of power between the CCP and the government so that there would be less overlap of political authority and more accountability for each. He supported the creation of a new civil servant system that emphasized professional skills rather than just political loyalty.

Deng's political reform was significant but inherently limited. He had no intention of moving China from a Communist system to a Western-style democracy (which he often equated with chaos). He made it clear from the very beginning that he would not tolerate anyone who tried to mount an organized challenge to Communist rule—and his actions consistently demonstrated his determination in this regard. Deng was responsible for the hard-line policies that helped crush the Democracy Wall Movement of the late 1970s, then the student demonstrations in 1985 and early 1986, and finally the massive 1989 student uprising. Deng justified these crackdowns on the grounds that China's economic modernization depended on stability, which he maintained was directly threatened by these movements.

Nevertheless, once the door to political reform had been opened, not even Deng and his successors could completely close it. Since the 1989 crackdown, the Chinese government has taken numerous actions to tighten its control, including some rather harsh treatment of political dissidents and social or spiritual groups that supposedly pose a threat to the regime, such as the Falun Gong movement. In a sense, however, the Chinese government has become a victim of its own successes. As the public gained more wealth and freedom in the wake of the reform, they also became more assertive in pressing for their rights, protecting their interests, trying to hold government officials accountable for their performance, and seeking new venues to express themselves. Democratization thus gained a toehold even though the formal political system remained unchanged. The pace of political change has been slow, the process tortuous and characterized by uneven results. But the overall trend is unmistakable: China has been moving away from its old authoritarian system and closer to democracy.

Rights in China Today

Democracy is ultimately built on individual rights and freedom. So just how much has the ordinary Chinese gained in these areas in recent years? The answer is both a lot and very little. In terms of personal freedom, the changes are quite impressive. Under the reforms, the Chinese have gained the right to choose where to live, although the state still denies permanent residency for peasants in

the cities (a few localities such as Shenzhen have recently abandoned these restrictions). The Chinese are now free to pursue employment opportunities as they wish. They are also free to travel much more widely, as the government has relaxed restrictions on international travel.

Activists assail China's human rights record in Tibet during a march in Vancouver, Canada. Chinese leaders bristle at such criticism, but many outside observers say that human rights abuses in China remain common.

In terms of political rights, the picture is much less encouraging. In theory, the Chinese constitution guaranteed freedom of speech, association, and religion even before the recent reforms. In reality, a series of government-imposed restrictions rendered these guarantees largely meaningless. Still, the government has been unable to stifle all criticism, and occasionally it has even been forced to bend to massive public pressure for change. Ironically, this has sometimes resulted from a by-product of China's economic reform and opening up to the outside world: the expanded flow of information made possible by the introduction of modern communications technology, including the Internet and text messaging via cellular phones. A tragic episode that occurred in 2003 is quite telling.

In March of that year, police stopped a 27-year-old graphic designer on a street in the southern city of Guangzhou. Because he was not carrying identification, the man was locked up in a local detention center for "repatriating" rural migrants found in the city without proper ID, a job, or a stable income. (He actually did have a job and resided in Guangzhou legally, but he had left his identification papers at home.) At the detention center the young man was beaten to death. A local court ruled the death a suicide despite the physical evidence indicating otherwise. As news of the incident spread on Internet chat rooms and bulletin boards (and even in the local press), numerous Chinese citizens expressed their outrage and demanded an investigation. Three young law professors from Beijing presented a petition before the Standing Committee of the National People's Congress (NPC). They argued that the regulations on detention, drawn up many years earlier, contradicted the provisions on personal rights contained in the Chinese constitution. Their argument struck a deep chord among a public fed up with police brutality and arbitrary power. Many joined the call. Under pressure, the NPC eventually decided to change the regulations on detention and order that detention centers be reorganized; in addition, several people involved in the killing of the young graphic designer were tried and convicted.

China's progress in the area of human rights is much debated. International human rights organizations and activists routinely criticize China's record on human rights. Their focus, of course, is on the political rights normally accorded to individuals in Western democracies. The 2010 annual report on human rights issued by the U.S. State Department, for example, offered this assessment of human rights conditions in China:

> A negative trend in key areas of [China's] human rights record continued, as the government took additional steps to rein in civil society, particularly organizations and individuals involved in rights advocacy and public interest issues, and increased attempts to limit freedom of speech and to control the press, the Internet, and Internet access. Efforts to silence political activists and public interest lawyers were stepped up, and increasingly the government resorted to extralegal measures including enforced disappearance, "soft detention," and strict house arrest, including house arrest of family members, to prevent the public voicing of independent opinions. Public interest law firms that took on sensitive cases also continued to face harassment, disbarment of legal staff, and closure.
>
> Individuals and groups, especially those seen as politically sensitive by the government, continued to face tight restrictions on their freedom to assemble, practice religion, and travel.

On the other hand, the Chinese government, along with the governments of a number of developing countries, argues that the definition of human rights should include the right to survival and economic development. By that barometer at least, China has made substantial progress.

It should be noted that even in the more conventional areas of human rights, some progress has been made. Chinese mistreated by the state apparatus now have a number of remedies available, including a law allowing citizens to sue a particular government agency if they can prove that they were harmed by "state action." In 2001 more than 100,000 cases involving administrative

北京高级法院强令我
所购买珠海格力公司
制、售的伪劣产品并
自行修复天理难容！

(该产品售价 160 万
元。格力公司安装、调
试期间便故障重复，并
书面承认其修理不好。)

可怜！当兵二十年（转
业时为正营级）竟被北京法
院枉法舞弊害得倾家荡
产、衣食无着、不得不
沿街乞讨。

可恶！腐败发展到法
院有法不依、知错不改
审非所诉、隐瞒证据、
釜底抽薪、执行不作为。

朝阳法院二中院审
理我公司诉不法台
两退货、返还货款合
同案时弃当事人要
后依法订立的此合
同而不审、它们隐瞒
证据、釜底抽薪、审
非所诉、心黑手毒。

Although confidence is growing in China's relatively young legal system, many people—including these two protesters outside a court in Beijing—remain frustrated with the system's limitations. China's justice system is criticized for its lack of independence from the government and the Communist Party, as well as for widespread corruption by judges and prosecutors.

disputes went to court. In March 2004 China amended its constitution to include the pledge that the state would "respect and protect human rights."

The Rule of Law

Establishment of the rule of law was one of the few areas in which a precondition for democracy seemed to overlap with the interests of the Chinese government. It is therefore not surprising that the progress made in this area has been most visible, substantial, and far-reaching.

The first signs of progress were the numerous laws that have been adopted in China. When China started its reforms in the late 1970s, the country lacked statute laws (laws established through enactment by a legislature) in virtually every category, including such essential elements of a functioning legal system as the civil and criminal codes. Over the succeeding years, China has enacted more than 450 laws. While there are still critical gaps in the country's basic legal framework, these laws form the backbone of a legal system that is by and large functional.

Another sign of progress can be seen in the public's changed attitudes toward the legal system in general. Recent studies show that growing numbers of Chinese believe that the law can protect their interests—and many are beginning to use the legal system for that purpose. Among the cases that have attracted significant public interest are civil cases involving such issues as medical malpractice and lawsuits involving business disputes. From 1990 to 2001, for example, the number of cases involving economic disputes almost doubled, from 591,000 to 1,149,000. In the last few years, there has also been an increase in the use of the administrative law to sue local officials for abuse of power or for negligence in carrying out their official duties. The number of such lawsuits increased from 35,000 in 1998 to more than 43,000 in 2002. As Randall Peerenboom, a law professor at the University of California at Los Angeles who has written frequently about legal issues in China, points out, "Rule of law is a function of institution building and the creation of a culture of legality." China has been advancing on both fronts.

A third sign of progress is the quantitative and qualitative improvement in the legal profession. China had no registered lawyers until the mid-1980s. Since then, the number of full-time lawyers, who have to pass vigorous nationwide bar exams, has risen sharply. In 1998 there were only 52,000 lawyers; by 2009 the number stood at 190,000. In addition, the Chinese government has allowed several hundred foreign law firms to open branch offices in China since the mid-1990s. Though the government has restricted the fields in which the foreign firms can practice, the introduction of legal concepts common in the West has nevertheless had a positive effect on the development of the legal system in China.

By contrast, progress in professionalizing Chinese judges and procurators lags behind. Because China does not use a jury system, judges' lack of experience and training can be particularly detrimental to the overall quality of the legal system.

Legal advances have been made at the provincial and local level, a development that has often been overlooked by outside observers. While the passage of laws is the responsibility of the National People's Congress, people's congresses at the provincial level may pass local regulations to enforce those laws. This arrangement has boosted legal reform in China in two ways. First, the ability of the provinces to pass local legal regulations sped up the process of enacting laws that were urgently needed but slow in coming from the national government. Second and more important, provincial legal regulations often allowed local governments to advance the legal procedures beyond the original laws. For instance, after the NPC passed the Organic Law of Villagers' Committees in 1998, a number of provinces passed local legal regulations to interpret how village elections should be held. In most cases, these local regulations made the election process more vigorous, and hence more meaningful. The regulations issued by Fujian Province, for example, included a requirement that the results of the pre-election auditing of village government be made public. Such institutional designs, though small, could go a long way to ensure the democratic nature of village elections.

Finally, with China's expanded role in the world and the increased integration of its economy with the world economy, Beijing has decided not only to participate more fully in international organizations but also to conform to international norms. As a condition of its entry into the WTO, for example, China accepted various legal and commercial obligations. While there is no guarantee that China will always abide by the agreements or treaties it has signed, the presence of international legal norms is in itself a major step forward in securing the rule of law in China.

There are still numerous limits on the rule of law in China, however. The most fundamental issue is how to apply the rule of law to the power of the CCP. Additionally, the central government's ability to impose its legal authority on local officials is not unlimited. Many local officials have blatantly and repeatedly refused to subject their power and decisions to the very laws the central government has enacted. Still, something is better than nothing. In the "long march" toward the rule of law in China, the process is perhaps as important as the results.

Competitive Elections

In the area of free elections, several seemingly promising trends emerged in China during the last decade of the 20th century and the first years of the 21st. Village elections were first held on a large scale in 1988, when the NPC passed the trial version of the Organic Law of Villagers' Committees. By 2000, village-level elections—some competitive and some less so—had become routine. In the meantime, Buyun township in Sichuan Province had experimented with the first direct election of a township executive. Elections in other townships would follow.

Many observers believed that these developments signaled Beijing's commitment to fundamental electoral reform. These observers predicted that democracy would gradually be extended upward, to the national level. Today, that scenario seems highly unlikely, at least in the near term. "The initial prediction that China had made a plan to begin direct and competitive elections at the bottom and slowly move elections up the chain," noted a 2009 report from the Atlanta-based Carter Center, "is incorrect."

China's national government has emphatically blocked democratization above the township level. Not only that, but many observers question how meaningful township- and village-level elections really are. In most cases, voters' choices are limited to candidates that have already been vetted by Communist Party officials.

The Chinese constitution defines the National People's Congress as the "highest organ of state power." The NPC's wide-ranging powers include electing China's president, confirming the premier (who is selected by the president), approving cabinet members, enacting legislation, reviewing and passing the state budget, and overseeing the operations of the central ministries. Since the beginning of the recent reforms, NPC members have, in theory, come to office through a process with elements of participatory democracy. That is because NPC members are elected by members of local people's congresses, and Chinese citizens may vote in people's congress elections (held every five years) at the county or urban district level. In reality, the notion that the NPC was even remotely a representative body was, until recent years, pure fiction, because the local people's congresses were themselves not representative—the CCP strictly controlled the nomination and election process.

Chinese farmers wait in line to vote during direct elections for the village committee at Hua Du, Guangdong Province.

A Chinese man walks by a government election poster after casting his vote in a local legislative election in Beijing

Several recent changes point to a somewhat greater level of participation in local people's congress elections. For example, while the laws always allowed citizens to directly nominate candidates (providing they collected at least 10 valid signatures), this provision was not seriously invoked until recently. Since the 1995 revision of the election law, a growing number of candidates for people's congress at the county or urban district level have been directly nominated by the voters (as opposed to the CCP or other social organizations) and actually elected. For example, in 1998 in Shandong Province, 40 percent of the final candidates for local people's congress were nominated directly by citizens. Of that group, about half were actually elected.

There have been no similar changes in NPC elections. Still, several interesting and potentially significant changes in the operation of the NPC have been observed. For instance, there have been efforts to turn some of the members of the Standing Committee (the NPC's executive body) into full-time members so that they might more effectively discharge the responsibilities of the NPC. (The full NPC, which has about 3,000 members, meets for only about two weeks each year.) In addition, a few members of the NPC have sought to highlight their links with local constituencies. A member from Zhejiang Province became one of the first to use her own money to set up a staff office so that she could more effectively solicit comments and suggestions from local voters. Her actions created a sensation in China. More important, members of the local congresses and the NPC have in recent years become more assertive in exercising their power in spite of the wishes of top CCP and government leaders. Occasionally government nominees have been rejected or endorsement of official reports has been withheld.

China still has a long way to go to have free, fair, and competitive elections. But democracy advocates hope the country will eventually build on the first small steps that have been taken.

Civil Society

A precise and universally accepted definition of *civil society* is illusive, but in general the term refers to the totality of institutions, organizations, and groups that exist independent of the state and the family and that, broadly speaking, are concerned with promoting social development and the public interest. Civil society would include, for example, charity organizations; professional associations; labor unions; consumers' rights organizations; human rights advocacy groups; conservation or environmental watchdog clubs; cultural, religious, and social groups; and women's groups. Such groups, in representing and advocating for a variety of interests and in providing forums for healthy public discourse, effectively constrain government authority. For this reason, the existence of civil society is considered essential for a functioning democracy.

Civil society in China is currently lacking, as the state for decades stifled the development of independent civic and social groups. Still, recent trends lead some observers to conclude that the emergence of civil society in China is not completely out of the question.

For one thing, there was considerable growth in the number of non-governmental organizations (NGOs) in China during the first decade

赞成　2082票
反对　586票
弃权　228票

A screen shows the results of a vote by delegates to the National People's Congress (NPC). The NPC is considered the "highest organ of state power," but in 50 years the assembly has never opposed a proposal by the Communist Party–dominated government.

of reform. (According to one study, the number of national social groups grew by 16 times, and the number of local social groups by more than 33 times, in the period 1978–1989.) But after the unrest of 1989, the Chinese government imposed stricter registration procedures for social groups. As a result, the number of registered social groups declined. However, the influence of the social groups was clearly on the rise. Some of the better-known groups, such as the National Consumers' Association, China Youth Development Foundation, and China Charity Federation, were pivotal in galvanizing the public for a particular cause or pressuring the government to take a particular action.

China has a large number of groups that are active but not registered with the government. Before the re-registration drive of the 1990s, there were an estimated 700,000 "people-run" organizations. After the drive, only 82,000 remained registered. Most of them either went underground or simply continued to operate openly without official registration. Such groups are active in a number of areas, from hobbies, education, and environmental protection to popular or folk religion.

A related development is the increasingly important role played by business associations and business groups (some of which are closely supervised by government agencies, others of which have significant autonomy). For example, to protect against charges of unfair business practices leveled by foreign countries, Chinese firms have increasingly formed strategic alliances; these alliances may lobby local officials or fight lawsuits overseas.

The role of trade unions in China has been more ambiguous under the reforms. In 2002, according to official statistics, there were 1.7 million grassroots unions with a total membership of 145 million and 47,000 full-time staff members. However, Chinese unions have never been independent. They are subject to strict control by the CCP and the state; in fact, they serve as an extension of the government by providing government-mandated services such as care for retired employees. As such, the unions can hardly be classified as civil groups. Nor are they effective champions for Chinese workers. In

Chinese president Hu Jintao casts a vote on constitutional amendments during the closing session of the National People's Congress, March 2004.

Tens of thousands of Hong Kong residents march to protest the growing gap between the wealthy and the poor in China, July 1, 2011. The government allows residents of this semiautonomous city certain freedoms not available to other Chinese, including the right to hold public protests.

a recent survey, more than 52 percent of the workers felt that their power in the factories had been in decline under the current reform. Only 9 percent of those surveyed thought that the unions were "capable of protecting their interests."

However, there have been some changes in the role of unions in recent years. For example, unions have assisted members in filing lawsuits or providing logistical support during labor disputes. Similarly, as more and more foreign and overseas companies have established operations in China, the demand for protecting workers in these companies has also risen. Unlike SOEs or domestic companies, which are subject to extensive government regulations, some of the overseas firms, particularly those run by Taiwan and Hong Kong businessmen, do not provide adequate protections and benefits for their employees such as workers' compensation, unemployment insurance, or a safe workplace. As a result, many workers have turned to the unions for help, and several local governments have recently pushed for a labor union presence in foreign-owned companies.

As is apparent from the preceding discussions, China's political reform has been full of contradictions. Some old authoritarian practices remain intact or, in certain cases, have been reinforced by a government fearful of losing its control. At the same time, beneath the formal power structure and the appearance of a one-party dictatorship, change has already shifted much actual authority and influence toward various emerging institutions and groups. In today's China it is possible to discern a general trend toward a more open political system with an increasingly diverse distribution of political authority and resources.

Deng Xiaoping and U.S. president Jimmy Carter sign a treaty officially normalizing relations between their respective countries, January
1979. Although frictions in the bilateral relationship have flared up
periodically, U.S.-China cooperation is considered crucial by both
Washington and Beijing.

6

Reform and U.S.-China Relations

The ripple effects of China's reforms have reached far beyond its borders and spread into its relations with other countries. As the world's largest economy and only superpower, the United States has a huge stake in where reform leads the world's most populous nation, which is emerging as a major player on the international stage.

An Important but Uneasy Relationship

The United States had no official contact with China until President Richard Nixon's historic visit to China in 1972. On January 1, 1979, the United States and China officially normalized their diplomatic relations. Since then, the U.S.-China bilateral relationship has grown by leaps and bounds. On the other hand, there are still many areas in which the two nations do not always see eye to eye.

Before the Cold War wound down in the late 1980s, the United States and China built a de facto alliance against what each perceived as Soviet expansionism. After the 1989 Tiananmen massacre, which came just two years before the collapse of the Soviet Union, the United States began to restrict its strategic relationship with China. In addition to imposing sanctions on China, the United States voiced criticism of China's handling of a whole set of political and security issues, ranging from China's human rights record to its treatment of Tibet to its posture regarding Taiwan.

Despite these frictions, the United States and China maintained close and frequent contact at the highest levels because each nation realized that cooperation on regional and international issues was vital to its national interests. For example, the United States viewed China as a key ally and critical player in keeping peace on the Korean Peninsula. Not only did China retain significant influence over North Korea through its aid programs, but China also shared the U.S. goal of keeping the peninsula free of nuclear weapons. China, for its part, has in recent years switched from a rather passive stance to assuming a leading role in resolving the crisis over North Korea's development of nuclear weapons. Beijing hosted six-party talks among the nations with the most at stake regarding nuclear proliferation on the Korean Peninsula: North Korea, South Korea, the United States, Japan, and Russia, in addition to China. As of early 2012, however, the situation remained at an impasse, and North Korea was already in possession of at least a few nuclear warheads.

The United States has long pressed China to take more aggressive steps to prevent the spread of weapons of mass destruction (WMD), which include chemical and biological weapons in addition to nuclear weapons. Chinese cooperation is essential because China has been a major exporter of dual-use technology (technology that can be used for both military and civilian purposes). U.S. policymakers suspect some of the countries that have received such technology from China of seeking to develop WMD programs. Under U.S. pressure, China has in recent years taken a number of steps to curb WMD proliferation, including the signing of international agreements designed to limit the transfer of missile technology and the issuing of stricter internal regulations on export licensing of materials and equipment that could be used for the development of WMD.

The September 11, 2001, terrorist attacks on New York and Washington, D.C., highlighted another area in which the United States and China share common interests. In the wake of the attacks, the two nations have worked closely on key aspects in the global fight against terrorism, including information sharing and political and financial support for the rebuilding of Afghanistan.

Negotiators from the United States, Japan, China, North Korea, South Korea, and Russia begin talks on the North Korean nuclear crisis in Beijing's Diaoyutai State Guesthouse, February 2004. In recent years China has taken a leading role in attempting to resolve the crisis.

But several hot spots in U.S.-China relations still have the potential to erupt. Among the most prominent is Taiwan, where a growing independence movement has provoked sharp warnings from Chinese leaders; China has said that it reserves the right to use force to reunite Taiwan with the mainland should the Taipei government formally declare its independence. Interestingly, economic ties between Taiwan and Mainland China have grown substantially in recent years: more than 30,000 Taiwanese companies now do business in Mainland China, with investments exceeding $30 billion. Tens of thousands of Taiwanese now live in Shanghai, Beijing, and other mainland cities. Yet the two sides remain in a state of perpetual tension over the current and future status of the island. The United States has, since the early 1970s, recognized the "one-China" principle (that Taiwan is part of China). But U.S. law also obliges Washington to provide Taiwan with arms, and in April 2001 President George W. Bush even stated that the United States would "do whatever it takes" to defend Taiwan in the event of a Chinese attack—which caused much consternation in Beijing. Clearly, the Taiwan–Mainland China issue is rife with risks, and any miscalculation in Washington or Beijing could easily do serious, perhaps even fatal, harm to the U.S.-China relationship.

Compared with the political and strategic relations, economic links between the United States and China have grown much faster and yielded more concrete benefits for both sides. In 1978, the year the United States normalized its relations with China and China adopted its open-door policy, trade between the two countries was a mere $1 billion. By 2011, U.S.-China bilateral trade stood at more than $500 billion, making China the second-largest trading partner of the United States.

Other economic ties have also flourished. But all is not well in the economic relationship between the United States and China. From the U.S. perspective, there are at least three large problems: a huge trade deficit with China, which reached almost $300 billion in 2011; growing U.S. complaints about unfair trade practices, including China's currency policy; and the lack of legal protections for U.S. companies doing business with China, particularly lax Chinese efforts to prevent the violation of intellectual property rights. The Chinese, on the other hand, have complained about U.S. restrictions on the export of high-tech products to China. (China has also argued that U.S. trade deficit figures are exaggerated.)

In addition to trade, cultural ties have also advanced substantially. China welcomes more than 2 million American visitors annually, and U.S. films and television programs are quite popular in China. A fast-growing number of U.S.-based educational institutions, non-governmental organizations, and even religious groups have established a presence in China. For its part, China sends thousands of students to the United States annually. And hundreds of thousands of Chinese tourists have made the United States a destination. In fact, at some U.S. landmarks Chinese visitors are so abundant that security guards have learned how to greet them in Chinese!

Reform and the Future of U.S.-China Relations

China's reforms have produced a booming economy and a more open society. These two factors and changes in the international and regional environment form a basic foundation on which the ties between the United States and China have grown substantially and momentously. However, the rise of China poses another kind of challenge to the United States: Will a more powerful China be a threat or an opportunity?

Some in the United States have called for a new containment policy against China. They worry that the growing power of China could one day be used against the United States. They believe that a conflict with China is inevitable given the geopo-

Sailors from the People's Republic of China look at a display as they tour the USS Arizona Memorial at Pearl Harbor, Hawaii. Growing numbers of Chinese are visiting the United States, while more American tourists are taking vacations in China.

litical calculations and the huge political and ideological gap that still separates the two nations.

Others want to engage China and promote China's full integration with the world. They see this as the only way to make China behave in accordance with international norms and get it to be more responsive as a rising power on key regional and international issues.

In the end, it is the outcome of China's reform that will most likely determine the future of U.S.-China relations. China still has a long way to go before it catches up with, much less surpasses, the United States as the most powerful nation on earth. Still, how China uses its newfound economic might, political influence, and, to a lesser degree, military power depends on how the nation defines its role in the world and its relations with the United States and the West.

In 1980 Deng, who started the reform process in China, was asked by a reporter whether "all in capitalism is so bad." Deng's response, in essence, provided a rationale for China's willingness to open its doors to the West:

> It depends on how you define capitalism. Any capitalism is superior to feudalism. And we cannot say that everything developed in capitalist countries is of a capitalist nature. For instance, technology, science—even advanced production management is also a sort of science—will be useful in any society or country. We intend to acquire advanced technology, science, and management skills to serve our socialist production. And these things as such have no class character.

More than 30 years later, China has gained mightily from internal reforms and external contacts, especially contacts with the West. The degree to which China continues this path toward more economic and political freedom will to a large extent decide whether U.S.-China relations flourish or face a crash.

Chronology

1976 Mao Zedong dies on September 9 at the age of 82.

1977 University entrance exams are reinstated after having been abandoned for more than a decade during the Cultural Revolution.

1978 Deng Xiaoping, who reemerges as a top leader during a CCP meeting in December, calls for reform and an open-door policy; he is named *Time* magazine's "Man of the Year."

1979 On January 1, China and the United States establish full diplomatic relations; the "Democracy Wall" Movement, which started in 1978, ends with a government crackdown and the arrest of several prominent dissidents; for the first time since 1964, the Chinese government allows a Catholic Mass to be celebrated; China and the United States sign a trade agreement on May 14 that allows the United States to grant China most favored nation (MFN) status, an issue that will be hotly debated in the U.S. Congress in the years to follow.

1980 Members of the so-called Gang of Four, the radical leaders of the Cultural Revolution—including Mao's wife, Jiang Qing—are put on trial for treason (they are ultimately convicted and receive harsh sentences); China establishes its first special economic zone (SEZ), in Shenzhen, Guangdong Province.

1981 The Central Committee of the CCP passes a resolution acknowledging that Mao Zedong made mistakes in his later years; nevertheless, the resolution asserts, 70 percent of the chairman's acts were good and only 30 percent were bad.

1982 The CCP decides to abolish life tenure for Party and government officials and formally approves the "Rural Household Responsibility System"; the National People's Congress ratifies a new state constitution on December 4.

1984 China opens 14 coastal cities to foreign investment, expanding on similar policies that previously applied only to special economic zones; Deng Xiaoping is named *Time* magazine's "Man of the Year" for the second time.

1985 The Chinese government decides to extend certain reforms, such as allowing market forces to determine the prices of some goods, to the cities.

1986 In December students calling for political reforms demonstrate in several Chinese cities.

1987 Hu Yaobang, general secretary of the CCP, is ousted for his failure to stop the student movement.

1988 The National People's Congress passes a law establishing elections to select members of local village committees.

1989 Student demonstrations, which break out after the death of Hu Yaobang on April 15, inspire a democracy movement that draws millions of supporters in Beijing and around the country; the violent government crackdown in and around Tiananmen Square on June 3–4 provokes an international outcry and sanctions against China; Jiang Zemin is elected general secretary of the CCP.

1992 In his last major public act, Deng Xiaoping tours southern China in January, calling for renewed efforts to accelerate economic reform.

1993 The CCP endorses the concept of a "socialist market system."

1994 China and the United States resume diplomatic contacts at the highest level, which the United States had suspended after the Tiananmen crackdown.

1997 Deng Xiaoping dies on March 17 at the age of 92; on July 1 Hong Kong is returned to China after more than 100 years of British rule.

1998 The National People's Congress passes the Organic Law of Villagers' Committees.

1999 China initiates a crackdown on the Falun Gong movement, which the government labels a dangerous cult.

2001 China officially enters the World Trade Organization (WTO)—the highest regulatory body for international trade—after more than 15 years of negotiations.

2002 In October, Hu Jintao replaces Jiang Zemin as general secretary of the CCP.

2003 Hu Jintao is elected president of China, and Wen Jiabao is confirmed as China's premier; the United States becomes China's second-largest trading partner, with China the third-largest trading partner of the United States (after Canada and Mexico).

2004 China revises its constitution in March; new clauses require the state to respect and safeguard human rights and to protect private property rights and citizens' rights of inheritance.

2005 China invites James Soong, head of the Taiwan's People First Party, to tour the mainland, marking a change in strategy in the country's effort to reclaim Taiwan.

2008 Beijing hosts the Summer Olympics.

2009 Ethnic violence erupts in the Xinjiang region.

2011 On the 90th anniversary of the founding of the Chinese Communist Party, President Hu Jintao issues a warning about widespread corruption in the government.

2012 Bo Xilai, the top Communist Party official in Chongqing, is brought down by a murder and corruption scandal.

Glossary

Buddhism—a religion founded in India and based on the teachings of Siddhartha Gautama (the Buddha), whose followers generally believe that suffering is inherent in life and that one can be liberated from it by mental and moral self-purification. Buddhism filtered into China during the third and fourth century A.D.

Chinese Communist Party (CCP)—the political party, founded in 1921, that has held power in China since the establishment of the People's Republic in 1949.

Confucianism—an ethical system, based on the teachings of the Chinese philosopher Confucius (551–479 B.C.), that underpinned social relations and governance in China until the 20th century and that continues to have significant influence today.

Cultural Revolution—a 10-year political campaign (1966–1976), launched by Mao Zedong in order to restore a revolutionary spirit to the Chinese people, during which students and ordinary citizens were called on to root out "counter-revolutionaries" and "capitalist roaders" in government and the Communist Party. The Cultural Revolution seriously undermined the Chinese people's faith in the state and caused enormous human and economic hardship.

dual-track system—a system adopted by the Chinese government in the mid-1980s to allow a market-based economic sector to coexist with the state sector; it was designed to expand economic reform into urban China but to avoid the backlash that would occur if the state sector was dismantled totally and immediately.

Falun Gong—a movement that combines the use of folk Buddhist discourse with healing exercises. Falun Gong (literally, "dharma wheel practice") became popular in

China in the mid-1990s, but the government banned it as a "cult" harmful to society after members staged several protests in Beijing in April 1999.

Great Leap Forward—Mao Zedong's disastrous campaign to jump-start China's economic growth by raising production through greater human efforts and the introduction of new, collective institutions such as the people's communes in rural China. Lasting from 1958 to 1960, the campaign severely disrupted China's economy and led to the worst famine in recorded history.

May 4th Movement—a cultural movement challenging the Confucian basis of Chinese society and calling for reforms; it originated with protests that broke out on May 4, 1919, mainly among intellectuals and students angered at provisions made at the Versailles Peace Conference concerning the disposition of German-held territory in China.

National People's Congress (NPC)—China's parliament, which has historically been nothing more than a rubber stamp for the decisions of the CCP (though some observers have noted recent efforts to make the body more responsive to popular demands and to give it greater power).

one-child policy—China's official population policy, which was adopted in the late 1970s and which encouraged (and sometimes coerced) Chinese couples to have only one child.

open-door policy—the program of reforms launched by Deng Xiaoping that reversed Mao's self-reliance policy and opened China to foreign trade, investment, information flow, and person-to-person exchanges.

Rural Household Responsibility System—a reform program under which Chinese peasants were allowed to lease land from the state and were given the responsibility for managing the land and using surplus produce as they saw fit.

Further Reading

Chen, Nancy N., et al., ed. *China Urban: Ethnographies of Contemporary Culture*. Durham, N.C. Duke University Press, 2001.

Fewsmith, Joseph. *China Since Tiananmen: The Politics of Transition*. Cambridge: Cambridge University Press, 2001.

Lampton, David M. *Same Bed, Different Dreams: Managing U.S.-China Relations, 1989–2000*. City: University of California Press, 2002.

Lardy, Nicholas. *Integrating China into Global Economy*. Washington D.C.: The Brookings Institute, 2002.

McGregor, Richard. *The Party: The Secret World of China's Communist Rulers*. New York: HarperCollins, 2010.

Marti, Michael E. *China and the Legacy of Deng Xiaoping: From Communist Revolution to Capitalist Evolution*. Washington, D.C.: Drassey's, 2002.

Murphy, Rachel. *How Migrant Labor Is Changing Rural China*. Cambridge: Cambridge University Press, 2002.

Peerenboom, Randall. *China's Long March Towards Rule of Law*. Cambridge: Cambridge University Press, 2002.

Perry, Elizabeth J., and Mark Selden, ed. *Chinese Society: Change, Conflict and Resistance*. London and New York: Rutledge, 2000.

Rein, Shaun. *The End of Cheap China: Economic and Cultural Trends that Will Disrupt the World*. Hoboken, NJ: John Wiley & Sons, 2012.

Stockholm Environment Institute. *China's Human Development Report 2002: Making Green Development a Choice*. Cambridge: Oxford University Press, 2002.

Internet Resources

http://www.chinatoday.com

Managed by InforPacific Development Inc. in Europe, this site provides comprehensive links to various aspects of Chinese society.

http://www.chinadaily.com.cn

News and views from the perspective of China's government.

https://www.cia.gov/library/publications/the-world-factbook/geos/ch.html

The CIA World Factbook's China page provides basic facts and statistics.

http://www.gio.gov.tw

Official website of the government of Taiwan.

http://www.hrw.org/doc?t=asia&c=china

Human Rights Watch monitors developments in China.

http://www.state.gov/p/eap/ci/ch/

This website from the U.S. State Department provides updated general information on key aspects of China.

Index

Numbers in **bold italics** refer to captions.

Picture Credits

Contributors

DR. ZHIMIN LIN received his undergraduate degree from Fudan University (1982), MPA from Princeton University (1985), and PhD in political science from the University of Washington (1993). He is currently associate professor of political science and chair of the Chinese and Japanese studies program at Valparaiso University. Dr. Lin's research interest focuses on Chinese politics and international relations in East Asia. He is the coauthor of two books, *Changing Central-Local Relations, Reform and State Capacity in China* (Westview Press, 1994) and *Provincial Strategies of Economic Reform in Post-Mao China* (M. E. Sharpe, 1998). He is currently working on two research projects: one on reform in China's Zhejiang Province, and the other on a comparative study of reform in China and India.

JIANWEI WANG, a native of Shanghai, received his B.A. and M.A in international politics from Fudan University in Shanghai and his Ph.D. in political science from the University of Michigan. He is now the Eugene Katz Letter and Science Distinguished Professor and chair of the Department of Political Science at the University of Wisconsin–Stevens Point. He is also a guest professor at Fudan University in Shanghai and Zhongshan University in Guangzhou.

Professor Wang's teaching and research interests focus on Chinese foreign policy, Sino-American relations, Sino-Japanese relations, East Asia security affairs, UN peacekeeping operations, and American foreign policy. He has published extensively in these areas. His most recent publications include *Power of the Moment: America and the World After 9/11* (Xinhua Press, 2002), which he coauthored, and *Limited Adversaries: Post-Cold War Sino-American Mutual Images* (Oxford University Press, 2000).

Wang is the recipient of numerous awards and fellowships, including grants from the MacArthur Foundation, Social Science Research Council, and Ford Foundation. He has also been a frequent commentator on U.S.-China relations, the Taiwan issue, and Chinese politics for major news outlets.